Saints

www.pocketessentials.com

Other Pocket Essentials by Giles Morgan:

Byzantium
Freemasonry
The Holy Grail
St George

Saints

GILES MORGAN

POCKET ESSENTIALS

This edition published in 2008 by Pocket Essentials
P.O.Box 394, Harpenden, Herts, AL5 1XJ
www.pocketessentials.com

Edited: Nick Rennison
Index: Richard Howard

A CIP catalogue record for this book is available from the British
Library.

ISBN 978 1 84243 238 9

2 4 6 8 10 9 7 5 3 1

Typeset by Avocet Typeset, Chilton, Aylesbury, Bucks
Printed and bound in Great Britain by J.H.Haynes Ltd, Sparkford, Somerset

'Hang on St Christopher on the passenger side
open it up tonight the devil can ride'

Tom Waits, *Hang On St Christopher*

Contents

Introduction

Saints and the concept of sainthood have had a dramatic and lasting impact on society. Their influence can be found in both profound religious contexts and within the secular everyday world in which their cultural presence often goes virtually unnoticed. For many people the saints serve as direct intercessors between themselves and God but it is arguable that, even for those without strong religious beliefs, they form part of an unconscious cultural tradition that is deeply embedded in the collective psyche. Although saints developed from, and are most closely linked to, Christianity there are clear parallels with many of the ideals and values that they represent in other world religions. Even more significantly, it is possible to find fundamentally similar concepts in a range of pre-Christian beliefs and religions. Put simply, the concept of the holy man or woman is an ancient one.

The word 'saint' is derived from the Latin term 'sanctus' meaning 'holy'. The earliest recorded saints were very often martyrs who chose to die for their faith during periods of religious persecution. The original meaning of the word 'martyr' was 'witness'. As I intend to argue in later chapters, our understanding of the meaning of these terms has undergone considerable change and development. Where once early Christian communities acclaimed individuals as saints because they had led particularly pious and spiritually devoted lives, today the process by which the Roman Catholic Church creates a saint is far more institutionalised and complex.

The earliest surviving written record of the veneration of an early Christian martyr relates how St Polycarp was prepared to die for his faith in 156 AD. Importantly the document also records that his fellow Christians gathered together his bones, which are referred to as 'relics', and placed them at a site where they could revisit them on the anniversary of his death. This is an early example of how Christians would gather together in remembrance of the individual to pray on their behalf. Soon the belief grew that the departed could act as a powerful intercessor between themselves and God. Over time the burial sites of such martyrs would become important shrines and centres of pilgrimage.

Christians would commonly celebrate the dates of death of such early martyrs as feast days rather than, for example, their dates of birth. This was because it was believed that the day of their martyrdom was the day on which they had won their 'crown' in heaven and been granted immortality through their selfless devotion to their faith. It has been observed that many aspects of the cults of Christian saints can also be found in pre-Christian traditions. For example, in the ancient Greek world the concept of a patron or localised god or goddess was commonplace. Perhaps most famously, the city of Athens was said to be under the protection of Athena whilst the celebrated sanctuary of Dodoni, close to the border with Albania, lay under the aegis of Zeus. Indeed, the practise of collecting the bones of ancestors together in sacred sites stretches far back into pre-history. At such sites tribal shamans or priests appear to have invoked the spirits of their ancestors as powerful mediators between humanity and their deities.

The spread and development of Christianity in Western Europe also served to create new saints and martyrs prepared to live and die for their faith as they attempted to convert often unwilling and aggressive peoples. In the British Isles, these include St Patrick, the patron saint of Ireland, and St David, patron saint of Wales. However, many other so-called Celtic saints also emerged during this period such as St Aidan who ranks amongst the patron saints of the important early Christian centre of Lindisfarne in Northumberland.

As has been noted, many other religions traditionally revere individuals of particular holiness or sanctity. Islam venerates many of the same figures as Christianity. A notable example is St John the Baptist whose shrine is located within the Ummayad Mosque. There are also similarities between the celebration of Christian saints and figures within Sufism who have important shrines and whose feast days are observed. The title of Mahatma within Hinduism carries many of the same connotations as that of saint.

The veneration of saints in Europe reached something of a pinnacle during the middle ages and this was reflected in the massive popularity of the collection of stories relating the lives of different saints known as *The Golden Legend*. This written work was compiled by Jacobus de Voragine and served to crystallise the many myths and legends that had become attached to a number of saints. During this same period it became the prerogative of the Holy See rather than localised popular acclaim to delegate the status of saint. Today, Innocent III (c. 1161–1216) is seen as the pope who established the right of the papacy to act as the ultimate authority on the granting of sainthood.

During the often violent upheavals of the Reformation, individuals on both Catholic and Protestant sides who were prepared to die as martyrs for their faith came to be viewed as saints. In England, the deposed monarch King Charles I came to be recognised in some Anglican traditions as a saint because of belief in the divine right of kings to rule.

The veneration of saints was carried to the new world and this often resulted in some unexpected and somewhat bizarre religious hybrids. Slaves in Cuba would merge their traditional beliefs with the cults of the saints to create a form of voodoo known as Santeria. In recent times, saints have continued to be created by different Christian Churches and include martyrs of the Spanish civil war and the murdered Romanov family in Russia.

Today the influence of saints can be found throughout the modern world in such commercial settings as the celebration of St Valentine's Day and in the role of St Nicholas as Santa Claus or Father Christmas. Their legacy is preserved within place names throughout the world and in their adoption by differing countries, professions and occupations. A study of the lives and varying patronages of saints and of their continuing roles both within the sacred and profane areas of our culture reveals much that is fascinating, admirable, compelling, disappointing and troubling in ourselves.

Early Christian Saints and Martyrs

Saints can be divided into two very broad categories. The first consists of the followers and relatives of Jesus who appear within the New Testament and the second of later post-biblical martyrs and saints. As we will see, the figure of the Virgin Mary has been of particular importance in Christianity and so too have the Holy Apostles. Interestingly, the role of Joseph is less important and the status he has been accorded has been a mixed one. The earliest post-biblical saints were generally martyrs who died for their beliefs under oppressive rulers and, in this chapter, there is a brief and selective survey of their lives and influence on the development of Christianity.

Mary, The Blessed Virgin

As the mother of Jesus Christ, the Virgin Mary occupies a unique place above that of all other saints. However, there has been controversy amongst Christians over the status that she has historically been accorded. In particular, the Roman Catholic Church has been criticised by Protestant theologians for elevating her to a role that at times seems almost to have eclipsed that of Christ himself. The claim that she was herself entirely without sin has also been disputed. The importance of Mary within Christianity is of particular interest in the context of a strongly patriarchal religion. It could be argued that her popularity as a saint is specifically because of her role as a mother figure. Many pre-Christian religions from a range of cultures featured powerful and important Goddess figures such as Hera, Athena, Artemis, Epona, Sulis and Brigit. It is interesting to note the enthusiasm with which Mary as a sacred mother figure has been embraced and it is arguable that this is because she fulfils an archetypal and ancient role within society.

The early life of Mary is not recorded within the bible but, according to the apocryphal Gospel of James, her father was called Joachim and her mother was named Anne. The story of Mary's conception and birth has remarkable parallels with that of the birth of Christ. Written in the second century, the Gospel of James relates that Joachim and Anna were an older couple who had been unable to have children. Joachim was said to have been a rich man. When Joachim took a lamb to the temple to offer it as a sacrifice it was rejected because he and his wife had never produced children. This rejection drove Joachim to walk into the desert where he joined some shepherds. Deeply hurt and disconsolate, Joachim experienced a miracle when the Angel Gabriel appeared to him and told him that his wife Anne would bear him a child. Gabriel instructed Joachim to travel to the Golden Gate of the city of Jerusalem where he would meet Anne. Gabriel had also appeared to Anne and told her to meet her husband there. When Joachim arrived Anne was standing under a laurel tree. He greeted her with a kiss and it is said that she then became pregnant with Mary.

As thanks for the miraculous pregnancy, Anne and Joachim agreed that their child would serve God. At the age of three, Mary was taken to the Temple where she stayed amongst other virgins and helped to make clothes for the priests. According to the Gospel of James, the marriage of Joseph and Mary was arranged through divine intervention. The High Priest of the Temple was visited by an angel who instructed him to find a husband for Mary when she was fourteen years of age. Following the words of the angel, the High Priest ordered a group of men to appear before him who were potential suitors and, according to legend, they were told to bring their walking staffs with them. Joseph from the town of Nazareth was a carpenter amongst the group of suitors. When the group was assembled before the High Priest, Joseph's staff is said to have blossomed miraculously, thereby signifying that he had been chosen by God as Mary's husband. An alternative version of this tale states that a dove landed on the staff of Joseph as the sign of his divine selection.

The most important event in the life of Mary as related in the New Testament is, of course, the Annunciation. In the Gospel of Luke, the Angel Gabriel is sent by God and appears to the Virgin Mary who is engaged to Joseph and living in the town of Nazareth. Gabriel's first words to Mary are 'Greetings, favoured one! The Lord is with you' (Luke 1: 28). He announces that she will conceive a child not by human means but through the Holy Spirit. The words that Gabriel spoke to Mary are the source of the phrase 'Hail Mary'. Gabriel tells her that the son to whom she will give birth will be called Jesus and that he will be a great king. Mary dutifully accepts the role that has been given to her by God, saying to Gabriel, 'Here am I, the servant of the Lord: let it be with me according to your word' (Luke 1: 38).

In the Gospel according to Matthew, Joseph is initially alarmed when he discovers that Mary is pregnant because, at this point, they are only engaged and not living together.

Initially, he plans to break off the engagement but he is prevented from doing so by a dream in which he is visited by an angel. The angel informs him that the child she is carrying was conceived by the Holy Spirit, that he should name him Jesus and that he will save his people from their sins. According to the angel, the birth of Jesus will fulfil the prophecy of Isaiah concerning a virgin who would conceive and bear a son. Joseph obeys the instructions of the angel and, furthermore, has no 'marital relations' with Mary until the birth of Jesus. The next important event in the life of Mary is referred to as the visitation. In the gospel of Luke, Mary makes a visit to her relative Elizabeth. Elizabeth is older than Mary and has never had children with her husband, a priest named Zechariah. However, the angel Gabriel has appeared to him and informed him that his wife will bear him a son who will be named John. He has also told Zechariah that his son will be a very significant and holy man who will proclaim the coming of Jesus.

Following the birth of Jesus, Mary appears intermittently during his adult life. She is present, for example, at the wedding at Cana. Most dramatically, she is present at the crucifixion at the base of the cross. In the Gospel of John, Christ commits his mother to the care of John, saying to her, 'Woman, here is your son' and to John, 'Here is your mother' (John 19: 26–27). One tradition claims that, following the death and resurrection of Jesus, Mary travelled to Ephesus on the western coast of modern day Turkey where she ended her days. Other non-biblical sources claim that she died in Jerusalem. Some traditions claim that an angel appeared to her three days before her death to announce that she would be taken into heaven. It is also said that all of the apostles were miraculously present at her death.

In a later theological development during the seventh century, the Church in both the East and West, in what is known as the doctrine of the corporal assumption, declared that Mary had been taken to heaven. Interestingly, this idea had been put forward previously in non-canonical apocryphal texts. In religious art, particularly that of the Roman Catholic Church, Mary is depicted as being crowned by Christ or the Trinity as the Queen of Heaven.

Interestingly, Joseph as the foster father of Christ has enjoyed less popularity as a Christian saint. To a certain extent, he was even slightly maligned and disrespected during the medieval period. Because he does not appear in the Gospel accounts of the crucifixion it was believed that he had died before that point in the life of Christ. Some apocryphal legends state that Joseph was older than Mary when they became engaged and that he died with Jesus and his wife at his bedside. Because this was regarded as a peaceful and happy death, he is sometimes invoked by those who would like to reach a similar end. The insistence of the Catholic Church that Mary was a virgin throughout her life made Joseph something of a figure of fun, particularly in medieval mystery plays, but the gospels describe him variously as being 'just' and a 'righteous' man. In the modern era, his honesty and dignity in his life and work as a carpenter have led to the adoption of his feast day on 1 May, known as the feast of 'Joseph the Worker', as the date for the celebration of International Workers' Day.

Such has been the devotion to Mary that the Second Vatican Council actually took pains to stress that her importance and significance lies in her relationship to Christ and her obedience and service to God. In other words, her veneration should never exceed that of her son amongst Roman Catholics. Mary is also considered to be a sacred figure by

Muslims because she was the mother of Christ whom they recognise as ranking amongst the important prophets.

Mary Magdalene

Perhaps no other Christian saint has been the subject of so much controversy in recent years as Mary Magdalene. She is revered as a saint in the Eastern orthodox, Roman Catholic and Anglican churches and is an important figure within the New Testament.

The name 'Magdalene' derives from 'Magdala', her town of origin. Her title simply means that she is Mary of Magdala. Her feast day is 22 July and, when she is depicted in religious art, her symbols commonly include an alabaster jar containing ointment. She is often portrayed with long, flowing hair, kneeling at the base of the cross upon which Christ was crucified.

In later Christian traditions, Mary Magdalene is commonly referred to as a prostitute and she is described as being the patron saint of penitent women. However, the New Testament actually makes no mention of her being a prostitute. Since the discovery of the Gnostic gospels at Nag Hammadi, many writers and historians have speculated that Mary Magdalene's status and relationship with Jesus have been considerably altered by the Catholic Church in its later history. Many point to the tantalising evidence offered by the Gospel of Philip which appears to suggest that Mary Magdalene was the disciple who was actually closest to Jesus. The text describes her in Greek as being a 'koinonos' of Jesus. This term has been variously interpreted as meaning 'friend' or 'companion' but others have suggested that, in fact, it means that the two were lovers.

The Holy Apostles

St Peter

St Peter always appears first in lists of the apostles and has particular importance in the development of Christianity. He was a key figure in the life of Christ. His original name was Simon and he lived in Bethsaida, close to the Sea of Galilee. Like his brother St Andrew, he made a living as a fisherman. Jesus renamed him Peter because he had recognised that he was the messiah. In a key passage from the New Testament Christ addresses St Peter, saying, 'Blessed are you, Simon son of Jonah! For flesh and blood has not revealed this to you, but my Father in heaven. And I tell you, you are Peter, and on this rock I will build my church, and the gates of Hades will not prevail against it. I will give you the keys of the kingdom of heaven, and whatever you bind on earth will be bound in heaven, and whatever you loose on earth will be loosed in heaven' (Matthew 16:19). Interestingly, in the Gospel of St John, Simon is given the name 'cephas', the Aramaic term for 'rock', and the Greek equivalent of this is seen in his new name of Peter. Importantly, Christ predicted that, on the day that he was arrested, Peter would deny all knowledge of him three times before the cock crowed at the break of day. However, although it was St Mary Magdalene who first encountered Jesus outside the empty tomb in which his body had been laid, St Peter was the first of the apostles to whom Christ appeared.

St Peter is, of course, regarded as the first pope of the Roman Catholic Church. Because St Peter is seen as holding the keys to the gates of heaven and is commonly depicted in religious art holding a pair of keys, his patronage as a gatekeeper has often been invoked by Christians. An interesting example of St Peter's protection being sought in this way is the crusader castle dedicated to him which was built at Bodrum on the Southern Aegean coast of Turkey by the Knights of St John in 1402. Built on the site of a previous Byzantine fortress – which itself was located close to one of the wonders of the ancient world, the Mausoleum of Halicarnassus – the Castle of St Peter is a huge construction that controls the port around which the town is based. Although the crusader forces had lost the Holy Land by the time it was built, the Knights of St John continued to exert a powerful presence in the region from their base on the nearby island of Rhodes. Set into the wall above the gateway to the castle is a medieval sculpture of St Peter holding his customary pair of keys and it is clear that he is being invoked as a guardian for the defence of this stronghold against hostile forces.

St John

The apostle St John was the brother of St James the Great and, like St Peter, was a fisherman. Because St John and his brother were such ardent supporters of Jesus he called them 'Boanerges' which translates as 'sons of thunder'. In the New Testament both St John and St James the Great were present during the Transfiguration and at Christ's Agony in the Garden of Gethsemane. As Jesus hung on the cross, he commended his mother Mary to the protection of St John shortly before his death. Following the death and resurrection of Christ and his ascension to heaven, St John joined St Paul whom he served in spreading the word of Jesus. However, where all the other disciples were martyred for their faith, St John is unique in that he was said to have lived to an advanced old age. He is said to have been persecuted by the emperor Domitian but lived on and ended his days at the city of Ephesus in Anatolia, the ancient name for modern day Turkey.

In religious art St John is commonly depicted holding a chalice that contains a dragon or a serpent. This image derives from the story that a high priest of the cult of Diana at Ephesus challenged St John to drink from a cup containing poison. He did drink from the cup but survived unharmed and also resurrected two other men who had been killed by drinking from the same cup. His other attributes often include a book, symbolising his role as an evangelist, and an eagle. The eagle was chosen to represent St John because it was believed that his gospel soared the highest and was the most revealing. St John was once also credited with writing the Book of Revelation when he was staying on the Greek island of Patmos late in his life but this is now thought to be doubtful.

St Matthew

In the Gospels of Mark and Luke, St Matthew is called by the name of Levi. He was a tax collector who worked for the occupying Roman Empire, collecting taxes from the Jews. This is significant in that tax collectors were regarded as unclean and were treated with contempt. However, Jesus shared a meal with Matthew at his house amongst guests who included other tax collectors. He was criticised for this but responded by saying that he embraced sinners and offered them help.

Matthew became one of the apostles and an evangelist. There are three main traditions about the martyrdom of St Matthew. One tradition claims that he was killed whilst preaching in Ethiopia. Another claims his martyrdom took place at Tarrium in Persia and yet another states that he died at Tarsuana, located to the east of the Persian Gulf. He is variously described as having been put to death with a sword or a spear and he is often depicted in religious art with one of these emblems. Because of his profession his other main emblem is a moneybag.

St James the Great

The brother of St John and the son of Zebedee, St James the Great was the first of the apostles to become a martyr and die for his faith. He was present at the Transfiguration of Christ and during the Agony in the Garden of Gethsemane.

He was martyred by King Herod Agrippa who persecuted Christians as a means of winning favour with the Jews. Agrippa was the grandson of the King Herod who had set in motion the slaughter of the innocents when he learned of the impending birth of a future king in the form of Jesus. St James was beheaded with a sword and, consequently, this is one of the symbols associated with him in religious art. The centre of the cult of St James the Great is Santiago de Compostela in Spain. It was claimed during the seventh century that he had preached the gospel there and, in the ninth century, that he had in fact been buried there. During the Middle Ages, it was an extremely important centre for pilgrimage and only Rome and Jerusalem possessed greater spiritual significance to Christians.

The symbols most commonly associated with St James are the pilgrim's hat and staff and the scallop shell. These aspects of his cult date from the period in the Middle Ages when his shrine at Santiago de Compostela was such an important site of pilgrimage and these were the items commonly carried by pilgrims. The actual purpose of the scallop shell was to allow pilgrims to scoop up water to drink from streams or fountains which they came across on their journey.

St James the Less

There is some confusion about the actual identity of St James the Less. The title itself is intended to differentiate between the two apostles named James and otherwise has no real significance. Because a number of figures within the gospel are named as James, a number of traditions have arisen. He is sometimes identified with James the brother of Jesus, James whose mother stood by Jesus on the cross and also with the individual responsible for writing the Epistle of James. It has been suggested that St James the Less was the first Bishop of the Jerusalem Church and early Jewish writings refer to him as James the Just. Perhaps suitably, there is also confusion over the manner of his martyrdom. One tradition claims that the Sanhedrin – the powerful Jewish elite of which St Joseph of Arimathea, who donated his own tomb to Christ following the crucifixion, had been a member – sentenced him to be stoned to death and then grotesquely sawn into two pieces. It has also been claimed that St James the Less was martyred by being beaten with clubs. Therefore, in religious art, his emblem is sometimes a saw and sometimes a club. He was martyred in 62 AD.

St Bartholomew

In the Synoptic gospels of Matthew, Mark and Luke, Bartholomew is listed amongst the names of the apostles. However, in the gospel of St John, he is referred to as Nathaniel. It is widely accepted that the two are, in fact, one and the same. Bartholomew apparently means 'son of Tolmai'. Tradition states that St Bartholomew became a missionary in

India and Armenia. The circumstances surrounding his martyrdom are particularly grim as he is said to have been flayed alive at Derbend on the coast of the Caspian Sea. Some alternative versions of his martyrdom have him beheaded or crucified upside down. As is so often the case in religious art, the symbols that represent him relate to his martyrdom – a set of flaying knives. He has, by extension and perhaps rather bizarrely, come to be considered as the patron saint of tanners and leather workers.

During the eleventh century, his cult became popular in England when Canterbury cathedral was given one of his relics – an arm that was supposed to have been his – by Queen Emma, the wife of King Cnut. The well-known church of St Bartholomew at Smithfield in the city of London was founded in 1123 by a courtier of Henry I called Rahere. He built the church, together with a monastery and a hospital that are no longer standing, in order to give thanks to God for having spared him from a serious bout of malaria he had contracted whilst visiting Rome. In the Middle Ages, St Bartholomew also became the patron saint of cheese merchants because of the similarity between his symbol of the flaying knife and a cheese knife. He is the patron saint of Armenia and is also invoked against nervous tics.

St Thomas

In the Gospel of John St Thomas is referred to as Didymus but he is known by the other apostles as Thomas. He is, of course, most familiar as 'doubting Thomas' who doubted the physical resurrection of Christ. Instead he famously said, 'Unless I see the mark of the nails in his hands, and put my finger in the mark of the nails and my hand in his side, I will not believe' (John 20: 25–8). His moment of doubt and subsequent acceptance of the resurrection of Christ have significance within the Christian tradition of belief based on faith rather than simply what can be seen or directly experienced. Little is known about the evangelical work of St Thomas after Pentecost but one tradition claims that he travelled to India and that he was martyred with a spear. The location of his martyrdom is said to have been Mylapore, near Madras. It is also claimed that his relics were translated to Edessa in 394 AD, from there to the Greek island of Chios and then on to Ortona in Italy. A number of Gnostic texts have been attributed to him, including the Acts of Thomas, the Apocalypse of St Thomas and the Gospel of Thomas.

The remaining apostles are St Jude, one of the brothers of Jesus, St Simon, known as the Zealot because he strictly observed Jewish law, St Philip, who is prominent in the story of the feeding of the five thousand, and St Andrew who was the brother of St Peter. St Andrew is the patron saint of Scotland and was famously martyred on the X-shaped or saltire cross that is now his symbol. Lastly St Matthias is the thirteenth apostle who replaced Judas Iscariot when Judas betrayed Jesus for thirty pieces of silver.

St Paul

St Paul has had a huge and dramatic influence on the formation and development of the Christian Church, one that, arguably, has eclipsed that of all other Christian theologians. He is a figure who can divide opinion dramatically. For many he is a key architect of such Christian concepts as the achievement of redemption through faith in Christ and the idea that Christ is the eternal son of God. In fact, the fourteen epistles written by St Paul are longer than the Gospel accounts of the teachings of Jesus Christ himself. Born in 65 AD he was a for-mer Pharisee who had persecuted Christians and who had then undergone his dramatic 'road to Damascus' experience. His profession was that of tent-maker but, after his vision of Christ, he undertook the role of apostle to the gentiles. He carried out three missionary journeys to Cyprus, Asia Minor and Greece. Returning to Jerusalem, he became the target of Jewish extremists. As a Roman citizen, he was entitled to stand trial in Rome, a request that was granted to him. He was then famously shipwrecked on Malta whilst travelling and there he is said to have converted the Roman governor of the island, Publius, to Christianity. Publius became the first bishop of Malta and is himself now remembered as a saint.

In the biblical account St Paul was taken on to Rome where he was kept awaiting a trial in 62 AD. Tradition states that St Paul later travelled to Spain but, upon returning to Rome, he (together with St Peter) was sentenced to death by the Emperor Nero. As a result of another dubious right he gained from being a Roman citizen, he was then beheaded and, at the spot where his head bounced three times, three fountains are said to have appeared. For some, St Paul was a brave and tireless missionary whose teachings have influenced many theologians since but others have viewed him as a misogynist, a repressed homosexual and a religious extremist. Interestingly, St Paul uses the title 'saint' to refer to Christians both living and dead. Over time, as we have seen, the epithet of 'saint' came to refer more often to those who had been martyred for their faith and those who stood as good exam-ples of living lives directed by Christian values and beliefs.

St Polycarp

As already noted in the introduction, the earliest, reliable written record of the martyrdom and subsequent cult of a saint other than those of biblical figures is that of St Polycarp. Born in 69 AD, he was a disciple of John the Apostle and went on to become the bishop of Smyrna. He became a significant figure within the Orthodox Church through his criticisms of such Gnostic thinkers as Valentinus and Marcion. However, he is best remembered as a martyr who was prepared to give up his life in defence of his faith in Christianity. In 155 AD, anti-Christian feeling in Smyrna led to a mob seizing St Polycarp who made no attempt to escape. He was apparently interrogated about his beliefs and it was demanded that he deny Christ and make sacrifice to pagan gods. In answer to this, he is said to have replied, 'For 86 years I have been his servant and he has never done me wrong. How then can I blaspheme my king and saviour now?' (*A Calendar of Saints*, James Bentley, p.40).

He was then taken to the local amphitheatre and paraded in front of the crowd as a Christian who refused to abandon his beliefs. Many called for him to be thrown to the lions but it was decided that he would be burnt at the stake. In the event, he was first stabbed to death with a sword and then his body was burnt. Later, other Christians returned to the scene of his execution and gathered together his bones and then reverently gave them a Christian burial. His feast day is 23 February.

St Ignatius of Antioch

The life and writings of St Ignatius of Antioch, like the account of the life of St Polycarp, are regarded as providing a valuable link to the history of the early Christian Church. St Ignatius was a Syrian who was appointed as the bishop of Antioch in 69 AD. The most valuable information about his life that has survived dates to the persecution of Christians under the Roman emperor Trajan. St Ignatius was ordered to be executed in Rome for his faith and taken by Roman soldiers from Antioch to die in the capital of the empire. During his journey the saint wrote a series of letters, seven in total, to be sent to the early Christian centres of Tralles, Rome, Ephesus, Magnesia, Philadelphia and Smyrna. He met St Polycarp on his final journey and his letters asked the early church leaders to draw together in solidarity. St Ignatius died in 107 AD in the Coliseum of Rome where he was killed by lions. Importantly, St Ignatius declared in his letters that the Church of Rome should be regarded as being of particular importance amongst Christians. This was, of course, because it owed its origins to the work of St Paul and St Peter. Today his feast day is celebrated on 17 October in the Roman Catholic Church.

St Alban

The most famous of the early Christian martyrs to have died for their faith in Britain is St Alban. The chroniclers Bede and Gildas wrote that St Alban was martyred in 305 AD in the amphitheatre of the Roman town of Verulamium, today named St Albans after him. He was said to have been a Roman soldier or citizen who gave sanctuary to a Christian priest in his own home. St Alban was converted to Christianity by the priest who then baptised him into the Church. In order that the priest could escape, St Alban exchanged clothes with him and was himself then arrested by soldiers searching his house. He refused to make sacrifices to pagan gods and was ordered to be beheaded for sheltering and impersonating the priest. Just before he was executed he is said to have converted a Roman soldier to Christianity. It is also claimed that, after St Alban was beheaded, his executioner's eyes fell out of his head.

St Augustine of Hippo

The influence of St Augustine of Hippo on the development of Christianity has been dramatic and, at times, controversial. He was born in 354 AD in Algeria. His mother, who was named Monica, was a Christian, although his father was not. As a young man he travelled to Carthage to train as a lawyer but abandoned the law in favour of studying philosophy. A major consequence of his studies was that initially he turned his back on Christianity and embraced Manichaeism. He further rejected Christian teachings by living with a mistress who bore him a child, a boy called Adeodatus.

After moving to Italy to teach in Rome and Milan he was drawn back towards Christianity and finally rejected Manichaeism after much soul searching. He was baptised in 386 AD and returned to North Africa two years later. He then embraced a monastic lifestyle and was ordained as a priest in 391 AD. In 394 AD he was appointed the coadjutor bishop of Hippo and, within a few years, took over the role completely.

The most controversial and criticised aspect of St Augustine's teachings has been his belief in predestination. According to St Augustine, those who had not been baptized were doomed to spend eternity in hell and he even included infants in that number.

He was also the first to suggest that sexual intercourse was the means by which original sin was passed on and was only acceptable as a means of procreation. His teachings on this subject were largely dismissed within the Christian Church, although clearly the suggestion has never been completely dispelled and has reared its ugly head in later movements such as Puritanism. During the Middle Ages a number of Christian orders embraced the Augustinian 'rule' which was founded on the basis of his teachings. These include the Austin Canons and the Dominicans amongst others. America's oldest city, St Augustine, is named after the saint because Spanish explorers landed at that point in Florida on his feast day of 28 August in the year 1565.

Saints in Eastern Christianity

The early Christian communities of the Eastern Roman Empire at times suffered terrible persecution under emperors such as Diocletian who ruled from 284 AD to 305 AD. These periods of oppression often led individuals to retreat into remote areas to practise their faith, and their lives and actions (as we shall see) proved to be an important influence on Christian philosophy and thought. However, Christians were to gain a new champion in the shape of Constantine the Great who ruled as sole emperor from 324 AD to 337 AD and is regarded as the first Christian emperor. The lives of the saints discussed in this chapter reflect the changing face of the Christian Church and the often-tumultuous events that they lived through and, in many cases, directly influenced.

St Anthony Abbot

St Anthony was born in the village of Coma or Koman in Upper Egypt in 251 AD and for this reason is often referred to as Anthony of Egypt. He is a particularly interesting figure within Christianity in that he was to influence prominent later Christians such as St Augustine and was extremely popular during the Middle Ages. He himself was arguably influenced by pre-Christian traditions and philosophers. According to the hagiographies that relate his life story, the parents of St Anthony were both Christians. When they died St Anthony was twenty years old and, in church one day, he is said to have been struck by the words of Christ in the Bible, addressing a rich young man. St Anthony clearly felt the passage had a meaning that was relevant to him and was soon to act upon it. The advice of Jesus had been, 'Go, sell what thou hast, and give it to the poor, and thou shalt have treasure in Heaven'.

Following this advice, St Anthony sold all his worldly goods and chose to live the life of an ascetic. He is said to have lived on a diet of bread with a small amount of salt and drank only water. He would not eat before sunrise and sometimes went days without drinking. His life followed a routine of prayer and fasting as he rejected all comforts and chose instead to sleep on a simple mat made from rushes or on the floor of his dwelling place. In search of greater solitude, the saint is said to have retired to a burial site in the desert and endured great temptations and hardships. Some stories have him tempted by beautiful naked women; others relate how he was attacked by the devil. Whilst the stories of St Anthony's time in the desert are often fanciful and melodramatic, it seems clear that he was a man undergoing inner conflict and turmoil as he strove to confront what he obviously believed were his own inner demons and failings. In search of an even more rigorous lifestyle on both the spiritual and physical levels, and perhaps in emulation of Christ, he travelled further into the wilderness in 286 AD to an abandoned fort that lay largely in ruins at Pispir on the eastern bank of the Nile. He is said to have remained there for the next twenty years, seldom seeing anyone, apparently involved in some tumultuous inner battle. At the end of this phase of withdrawal from the world he acted as a leader for a group of disciples who had been inspired by his example and founded some form of monastery. St Anthony is said to have made a living through mat-making and through working as a gardener and he encouraged his disciples to follow his example.

During the persecution of Christians by the Eastern Roman emperor Maxentius, St Anthony travelled to Alexandria to give support and courage to the Christian community. Although he appeared in public and wore a tunic of white sheepskin that symbolised his innocence and purity, he took care not to provoke trouble with the authorities and encouraged others to pursue a path of discretion. It is interesting to note that St Anthony appears, from surviving writings of the period, to have been familiar with philosophers such as Plato and to have absorbed them into his world-view.

One of the most dramatic events in the life of St Anthony occurred during the controversy over the so-called Arian heresy that plagued the early Church. Arianism was a divergent form of Christianity that was based on the theological viewpoint of an Alexandrian presbyter of the time called Arius. He put forward the philosophical argument that, if Jesus Christ had been created by God to bring salvation to the world, then necessarily there was a time when Christ the Son did not exist. If this was so, he argued, then God the Father was greater than Jesus Christ the Son. In recent years this has been interpreted as meaning that he concluded that Christ was simply a man. However, Arius did not dispute that Christ had been sent to the earth in order to die on the cross and so bring about the ultimate salvation of mankind. (It is also worth remembering that what is known of his beliefs is recorded in the works of his opponents.) St Anthony was requested by the bishops to travel to Alexandria to oppose the growing interest in Arianism. He argued against Arianism and is said to have changed the opinions of many and to have converted many.

This early pivotal theological dispute was to lead to the famed Council of Nicea and to the establishment of the Nicean Creed that still stands as a central point of belief within Orthodox and Western Christianity. The Nicean Creed teaches that Christ the Son is of the same substance as God the Father. The Council of Nicea took place in 325 AD and was presided over by Constantine the Great who later wrote to St Anthony, asking that he pray for his soul and recognising him as a renowned holy man capable of working miracles.

St Anthony is also said to have met St Paul of Thebes who is traditionally regarded as the first Christian hermit. St Jerome wrote an account of the life of St Paul of Thebes and relates that St Anthony met him in the desert. The meeting was said to have occurred not long before the death of St Paul. According to St Jerome, it was marked by a strange omen when a raven dropped a loaf of bread from the sky. Even more bizarrely, St Anthony is said to have requested that two lions should dig a grave for St Paul with their claws and is alleged to have buried him in a cloak that had been given to him by St Athanasius. St Paul died in 345 AD and is supposed to have been over 100 years old at his death. It has been suggested that he retreated to the desert to escape religious persecution. St Anthony is believed to have also lived a very long life, apparently dying at the age of 105 in the year 356 AD.

Although he was originally buried in an unknown location, in 561 AD it was claimed that his relics had been discovered and they were taken to Alexandria. Interestingly, in religious art, St Anthony is commonly depicted accompanied by a small pig and carrying a bell. The origins of this imagery do not derive from his lifetime but lie in the Middle Ages. It is claimed that the Order of the Hospital Brothers of St Anthony, or Antonines, possessed some of the saint's relics and kept them at Saint-Didier de la Mothe, which became an important centre of pilgrimage. They wore black robes emblazoned with the Greek letter Tau, or St Anthony's cross, in blue. When the members of the order called for alms in the streets, they rang bells as they went. They also had the unique right to let their pigs run free in the streets. These two aspects of the order and their connection to St Anthony were taken up by religious artists from that time onwards. A further connection between St Anthony and these two images can be found in the use of the word 'tantony' which, in English, can signify either the smallest pig in a litter or the smallest bell in a carillon.

St Pachomius

Another important figure within the history of the early Christian Church who was born in Egypt is St Pachomius. However, whilst St Anthony and St Pachomius shared the same religious creed, they were markedly and interestingly different in their approaches to religious life. St Pachomius is said to have been born to pagan parents in Upper Egypt and, as a young man, was forced to join the army in about 310 AD. According to the hagiographers, St Pachomius was taken by boat down the river Nile with other conscripted soldiers who were essentially prisoners. It is said that, during his journey, he encountered some Christians who, upon seeing that they were being held as virtual captives, gave the soldiers food and showed them kindness. Following his release from the army in 313 AD, St Pachomius became a Christian himself and was baptised. Initially, he lived as a hermit in the Theban desert. He had been inspired to do so by the example of an old hermit of whom he had heard called Palaemon who lived a life of great austerity. Eating a simple diet of bread and salt Palaemon also rejected the use of wine and oil as a permanent reminder of the sacrifice of Christ on the cross.

Eventually, however, St Pachomius turned what seem to have been exceptional managerial talents to the founding of monastic groups. He is said to have founded his first monastery in 320 AD on the banks of the Nile and, over the course of his life, he brought a further six monasteries for men into being. He is also said to have established a nunnery on the opposite river bank to the one on which the monasteries for men stood. These monasteries are said to have been substantial in size, occupied by thousands of monks, and St Pachomius' experience in the army is thought to have proved useful in their organisation. Monks were organised within them by their occupations such as baking or farming and the results of their labours were taken to the shops and markets of the city of Alexandria. Although Pachomius introduced a strict, military-style rule within the monasteries, monastic life was said to have been less extreme than that of some of the Christian ascetics dwelling in the desert who sought to grow closer to God through undertaking difficult and arduous lifestyles. The rule of St Pachomius was to influence such later figures as St Benedict and St Basil. His feast day is celebrated on 9 May and he is thought to have died in about 346 AD. In religious art, St Pachomius is often shown being carried on the back of a crocodile across the river Nile.

St Athanasius

St Athansius ranks as one of the most significant saints of the Eastern Church and is also greatly revered in the Western

Church. He was born in 296 AD into a Christian family and was educated in Alexandria. As a young man he became a deacon and also served as the secretary of Alexander the bishop of Alexandria. It was during this period of service under Alexander that St Athanasius became involved in fighting against the great heresy of Arianism that threatened to divide the early Christian Church. Both Alexander and Athanasius travelled to the critically important Council of Nicea in 325 AD in order to dispute the claims of Arianism and to champion the cause of Orthodoxy. Because of the part he played at this pivotal meeting St Athanasius gained a reputation that he was to maintain throughout his life as a champion of the Orthodox Church. However, his career within the Church was not an easy one even after he was appointed Bishop of Alexandria in 328 AD, following the death of Alexander.

Although the Council of Nicea and the formulation of the Nicean Creed seemed to put an end to the controversy over Arianism, Arius, the presbyter around whom the controversy had raged, still enjoyed the support of the mother and half-sister of the emperor, Constantine the Great. Many bishops within the Asian territories of the empire also supported his views and, in 327 AD, Constantine was persuaded to recall Arius from exile. Arius told the emperor that he accepted the Nicean creed and Constantine wrote to Bishop Alexander, suggesting that Arius be allowed to return to Egypt. Alexander refused to allow him to return and so too did Athanasius when he became bishop. As if his conflict with Arian sympathisers was not enough, Athanasius also found himself under attack from the Meletian Church. Led by their bishop, John Arkaph, the Meletian Church made a number of serious accusations against Athanasius, claiming that he was variously guilty of bribery, fraud and sacrilegious actions. Athanasius was cleared of all these charges but was finally accused of the murder of a Meletian bishop and of responsibility for having the victim's body cut into pieces. However, tradition claims that Athanasius was able to demonstrate the bishop in question was actually still alive and his name was cleared once again.

Undeterred, the Meletian Church went on to accuse him of rape. In this instance, the victim was apparently unable to recognise Athanasius as the man allegedly responsible whilst in court. In 335 AD Athanasius was summoned to the council of Tyre at the command of Constantine whose sympathies appeared to have moved towards the Arians. Once again Athanasius was met with accusations of impropriety, which he fought strongly against. When it became apparent that his accusers were intent on finding him guilty at all costs, Athanasius fled to Constantinople to seek the protection of the emperor.

Constantine was initially sympathetic but, when Athanasius was then accused of threatening insurrection in Alexandria if he was not reinstated as bishop, the emperor became furious. It was claimed that Athanasius was going to organise a strike amongst the port workers who loaded the ships with grain from Alexandria on which the city of Constantinople depended for its survival. He was banished to Tyre by the emperor. Events took a dramatic turn when Arius died suddenly of internal haemorrhaging in Constantinople but Athanasius was left in exile. He finally returned to Alexandria in 337 AD after the death of Constantine. Controversy continued to follow him for decades but, in the years between 365 and 373 AD, the Alexandrian church finally experienced relative calm. Athanasius ranks with Basil, John Chrysostom and Gregory of

Nazianzus as one of the Four Eastern Doctors of the Church. He died on 2 May 373 AD.

St Gregory of Nazianzus

Born in 329 AD, St Gregory was the son of the bishop of Nazianzus in the region of Cappadocia, today part of Turkey. At this time, it was a region within the territory of the Eastern Roman Empire in Anatolia. As the son of a bishop, St Gregory received an excellent education at the University of Athens. It was here that he met the future saint Basil the Great. He also studied alongside the young noble who would become better known to history as the Roman emperor, Julian the Apostate. After finishing his studies St Gregory became a monk at Pontus with his friend St Basil the Great. When his father reached the age of eighty, St Gregory returned to Nazianzus to help him in his work and in running the family estate. It was whilst he was helping his father that he was persuaded to become a priest, a role he had not previously been keen to embrace. Initially, the new life and responsibilities that he faced proved too much and he returned to Pontus. After ten weeks of turmoil, he finally decided to accept his new role and returned home again.

Although he suffered from poor health, St Gregory was called upon by the Orthodox bishops to help rebuild the Orthodox Church in Constantinople that had been persecuted by the pro-Arian emperor Valens. St Gregory faced much opposition from Arian Christians in his work but he began by turning his own house into a church. He worked tirelessly to promote the Nicean Creed against the beliefs of the powerful Arians and developed a reputation as an impressive theologian. St Gregory was a key figure in the Council of

Constantinople convened in 381 AD by the emperor Theodosius. This council reiterated the Nicene Creed and re-established, with the approval of Theodosius himself, that it was the official and accepted doctrine of the Church. Although the views of the Orthodox Church which St Gregory had represented were now the dominant force within Christianity, tensions still existed within Constantinople. St Gregory left the city believing that his work there was finished and returned to Nazianzus where he acted as bishop for a time. He later retreated from public work and offices and spent his later years pursuing study and writing poetry and his own life story. He died at Nazianzus on 25 January 389 AD. He is considered to be one of the four great Eastern Doctors of the Church.

St Basil the Great

It is clear that this well-known Eastern Christian saint was a member of a family with strong religious beliefs. He was born in 330 AD in Caesarea and his grandmother Macrina the Elder, his mother Emmelia, his father Basil the Elder, his brothers Peter of Sebaste and Gregory of Nyssa and his sister Macrina the Younger are all also recognised as saints. He enjoyed an excellent education at some of the best schools of the time including those of Athens and Constantinople. Whilst studying in Athens he met Gregory of Nazianzus. Both young men also met the future Roman emperor, Julian the Apostate, who abandoned Christianity and embraced the older pagan religious traditions of the ancient world, thus earning his famous epithet. Basil became a monk and spent time in both Syria and Egypt. In 358 AD he became a hermit at Neo-Caesarea.

However, in 364 AD, Bishop Eusebius of Caesarea requested the help of Basil and he abandoned his life of solitude. As previously noted, the Orthodox Church at this time was under attack from Arian Christians headed by the Emperor Valens. He was appointed as bishop of Caesarea in 370 AD. He worked to restore the Orthodox Church and to reiterate the Nicean Creed and preached the true nature of the Holy Trinity. However, he is also famed for giving away his personal wealth during a famine and personally helping to run a soup kitchen for the poor. Interestingly, Basil drew on his classical education, which would have included pre-Christian philosophies and beliefs, as a basis for his faith in Christianity. That is to say, he was open to ideas and innovations that were drawn from the non-Christian world and he is celebrated for his inclusive outlook.

St Basil the Great also established the rule for monastic life amongst monks and nuns in the Eastern, Greek and Russian Orthodox Churches that is still in use today. Basil stressed the importance of living a communal life, the importance of prayer and hard physical work. His philosophy focussed on living and working as a group rather than in pursuing a solitary and dramatically austere life. When he died on 1 January 379 AD, it is said that many, Christians and non-Christians alike, expressed sadness at his passing. In the Western Church he is numbered amongst the Four Greek Doctors who include St Athanasius, St John Chrysostom and St Gregory of Nazianzus. St Basil the Great is a patron saint of Russia, a country where he is an extremely popular and significant figure. He is also the patron saint of hospital administrators.

St John Chrysostom

Born at Antioch in 347 AD, St John Chrysostom became one of the most famous patriarchs or archbishops of Constantinople during the Byzantine period. His father was an officer in the army and Chrysostom received an excellent education within Antioch, at that time an important Eastern Christian city. He joined a Christian community based in the local mountains as a monk and lived a tough, simple and austere life with few luxuries, making his home in a cave. However, the damp and cold conditions in which he had been living damaged his health and he returned to the city of Antioch, becoming a deacon in 381 AD. Five years later, he became a priest. As the special assistant of the Bishop of Antioch he soon developed a reputation as a preacher. His abilities as a public speaker earned him the name 'Chrysostom' which, in Greek, literally means 'golden mouthed'. During the civil unrest in the Eastern Roman Empire which followed unpopular taxes introduced by the emperor Theodosius, his sermons are said to have been effective in restoring law and order. Chrysostom was chosen by the emperor Arcadius in 397 AD to become the new patriarch or archbishop of Constantinople and he was consecrated in the role in 398 AD by Theophilus, the archbishop of Alexandria. However, Chrysostom soon caused considerable disruption in Constantinople when he set about reforming the corruption he found within the court. He redirected money spent within the household of the patriarch to the care of the poor and sick and also tried to raise the moral standards of the clergy. Today, he is less positively remembered for his often ranting and vicious attacks on Jews and women.

He also earned many enemies at court after he criticised

the dress and make-up of important women. Indeed, such was the impact of his attacks that the empress Eudoxia believed that his comments were aimed directly at her. Matters took a turn for the worse when a statue of the empress, to which Chrysostom personally objected, was set up outside the church of Hagia Sophia. The empress, aided by a group of co-conspirator bishops, accused Chrysostom of referring to her as a 'Jezebel' and, claiming that he was guilty of treason, demanded that the emperor Arcadius have him banished. However, although the emperor complied with the wishes of the empress and had him banished, he was recalled to Constantinople almost immediately.

The empress had a change of heart after an earthquake which she believed was divine intervention for her scheming against the patriarch. Chrysostom refused to change his personal style, speaking out boldly against immorality and corruption where he saw it and it was not long before, in 404 AD, he was banished for a second time.

He died on 14 September 407 AD in Pontus, a distant region of the empire. Some believed that his death was the result of ill treatment he received from his guards. He was later reburied in Constantinople and today is numbered amongst the Four Greek Doctors by the Western Church. Within the Eastern Church, St John Chrysostom is one of the Three Holy Hierarchs and Universal Teachers. He is considered to be the patron saint of orators.

Celtic and Early English Saints

Christianity spread to Britain because it was a province within the Western Roman Empire. However, by 410 AD, the legions of Rome were leaving its shores as the Western Empire began to crumble. The power vacuum created by the retreating Roman occupiers left Britain exposed to raids and territorial incursions from waves of different incomers, including the Angles, the Saxons and, later, the Vikings. Communities in Britain faced difficult struggles for control with such invaders but, in Wales, Northumbria and Cornwall, Christianity was able to flourish. In 596 AD, Pope Gregory sent St Augustine to try to convert the largely non-Christian population of the south of England and he became the first Archbishop of Canterbury. The Celtic and early English saints discussed here tell not only the stories of individual Christians but also open an intriguing and often illuminating window onto the wider picture of British history in the post-Roman period.

St Patrick

Probably the most famous indigenous saint of the British Isles from the early history of the Church is Patrick, the fifth-century bishop who famously served as the apostle to the Irish. Although the exact location of his birthplace is not known, it is said to have been somewhere named Bannavem Taburniae in the west of Britain in the region between the river Clyde and the river Severn. His father was a town councillor who served as a deacon and who was himself the son of a priest. Famously, St Patrick was captured by members of an Irish raiding party who forced him to live as a slave in Ireland for six years. During his time in captivity Patrick became deeply religious and spent much time in prayer. According to legend it was revealed to him in a dream that he would escape his slavery and return home. It is uncertain whether he was set free or managed to run away from his captors but, after many difficulties, he did find his way back to his family. After his ordeal St Patrick trained as a priest.

Efforts had previously been made to convert the Irish by a bishop named Palladius but his mission had been generally unsuccessful. In around 435 AD, St Patrick was sent by the Church to Ireland where he set up his see in Armagh. One of St Patrick's primary aims in Ireland was to put an end to the pagan practice of worshipping the sun. Many of the prehistoric monuments of Ireland seem likely to have been linked to the concept of the sun as a form of deity, suggesting that this was a form of religious belief with extremely ancient roots. Newgrange burial chamber in the Boyne valley close to Dublin, for example, was designed with the specific intention that its inner burial chamber should be illuminated by the sun's rays at important times in the ritual year. Similarly, the megalithic stone circle of Beltany in County Donegal is orientated towards the May Day sunrise and the circle takes its name from the pre-Christian feast of Beltane celebrated at that time.

It has been suggested by some that the ancient Celtic Christian wheel cross takes its form from the meeting of

Christian and pre-Christian traditions. It has been conjectured that this integrates the Christian symbol of the cross with the pre-Christian solar wheel that may represent both the sun and the 'turning wheel' of the solar and agricultural year. However, it has also been argued that the style of the Celtic Cross has its origin in the much earlier Chi-Rho symbol which features the first two Greek letters of the name of Christ and which was surrounded by a circle. The first Celtic Crosses were made from wood and were gradually replaced by stone crosses. They marked places where preaching took place or served as commemorative monuments. These crosses, it is argued, were too tall to be encircled literally like the Chi-Rho symbol and so a modified circle was created around the crossing point.

Given that St Patrick set up his see in Armagh, close to the territory of a powerful king who was presumably sympathetic to his cause, it is interesting to speculate that the first Christian missionaries in Ireland had to use diplomacy and compromise to convey their message and that this is demonstrated in the wheel cross. St Patrick's 'battle' with the pagans (which may, in reality, have been more of an encouraging dialogue) is famously recorded in religious art and symbolism in images of the saint banishing the snakes from Ireland. The image of the serpent within different religious traditions is an interesting one, and many pre-Christian religions viewed the snake's ability to shed its skin as a miraculous act of re-birth and renewal. For Christians, however, from the serpent in the Garden of Eden onwards, the snake is a sinister and 'evil' creature linked to the devil. Therefore the imagery of St Patrick's victory over the serpent is likely to represent his triumph in converting a pagan population. St Patrick is also said to have demonstrated the concept of the Trinity – the Father, the Son

and the Holy Ghost – through reference to the three leaves of
the shamrock.

St Petroc

St Petroc is arguably one of the most overlooked saints of the
British Isles from the formative period of Celtic Christianity.
He is the patron saint of Cornwall and Devon although St
Michael and St Piran are also important saints within these
counties. Little is known with certainty about his life and
what records have survived have been disputed but he is
known to have lived during the sixth century. It is generally
accepted that he came from South Wales and some traditions
state, more specifically, that his father was King Glywys of
Glywsing, the ancient name for Glamorgan. His influence can
be determined in both North and South Wales through several
local place names. In North Wales the village of Llanbedrog is
dedicated to him and in South Wales St Petrox is named for
the saint. Variations of the spelling of Petroc are common.
Other Welsh sources name him as Pedrog whilst in English he
is sometimes called Petrock. French sources name him as
Perreux.

As a missionary spreading the Christian faith, St Petroc
travelled from South Wales by sea to Haylemouth. He founded
a monastery at Lanwethinoc that was re-named 'Petroc's-
stow' in his honour. This is the origin of the place name of the
Cornish seaside town of Padstow. Later in life, he founded a
monastery at the site of Little Petherick. He is famous for having lived as a hermit on Bodmin Moor and, in a story similar
to one told of St Giles, he is said to have protected a stag that
was being hunted. In religious imagery he is often shown with
a stag in memory of this event. It is interesting to note that a

number of hermit saints can be linked to wild animals in this way. Arguably, there are at least superficial parallels between them and pre-Christian sacred figures such as tribal shamans and Iron Age druids. In Celtic religions, Herne the Hunter or Cernunnos is depicted as an antlered god who leads the wild hunt whilst shamans often wore antler headgear during rituals and ceremonies. It may be that the symbolism of St Petroc and the stag has been influenced by, and acknowledges, older cultural traditions. Also, in western Christian iconography of the Middle Ages, Christ is often represented by a white stag. Other probably unreliable legends concerning St Petroc record that he was responsible for converting the pagan king, Constantine of Dumnonia, to the Christian faith. In one unusual legend, St Petroc is also said to have helped rather than harmed a dragon by removing a splinter from its eye.

When St Petroc died he was buried at Padstow. However, some time around 1000 AD, his relics, including possessions such as his bell and staff, were moved to Bodmin, which became his major shrine. In 1177, these relics were stolen by a Breton who carried them to the Abbey of St Meen in Brittany. The theft was brought to the attention of Bartholomew, Bishop of Exeter who, in turn, related the matter to King Henry II. The king ordered that the relics be returned to Bodmin but a single rib was left at St Meen. Today there are churches dedicated to St Petroc in Wales, Cornwall and Brittany whilst Devon has no less than eighteen named in his honour. His popularity in Devon is such that the flag of Devon is known as St Petroc's Cross and features a white cross with black edging on a green background.

St David

Although it is known that David lived and worked as a monk and bishop during the sixth century AD, the exact year of his birth is not known. He is most closely linked with South Wales and Pembrokeshire in particular. His current status as the patron saint of Wales began during the twelfth century and, in the Welsh language, he is known as 'Dewi Sant'. The earliest known written reference to St David is found in an Irish document called 'The Catalogue of the Saints' that dates from 730 AD. The text describes St David, Teilo and Gildas administering the mass to the Irish and also refers to St David as a bishop. Irish martyrologies dating from around 800 AD record that his feast day was held on 1 March and that his monastery was based at 'Menevia', an ancient name for St David's.

In 1090 AD, a 'Life of St David' was written by a man named Rhygyvarch although today it is not viewed as being wholly reliable. The author was the son of the then Bishop of St David's, Julien, and he wrote it with the aim of achieving Welsh religious independence from England. He describes St David as being the son of the king of Ceredigion. His father is said to have forced himself onto the mother of St David, St Non. According to Rhygyvarch, St David was actually born in extremely dramatic circumstances on top of a cliff whilst a violent storm was raging. The historian Geoffrey of Monmouth claimed that St David was actually related to the legendary King Arthur. It is stated in the 'Life of St David' that he was educated under St Paulinus in Carmarthenshire. He went on to found ten monasteries and was said to have instructed the monks to live like the monks of Egypt, devoting themselves to study and hard physical work.

They were also required to forgo meat and lived on a minimal diet of vegetables and water supplemented by bread. It is thought that he died in 598 AD and his feast day is 1 March. When depicted in religious art, St David is commonly shown dressed in his bishop's vestments, standing upon a raised mound with a dove on his shoulder. Although he is best known for his links with Wales, he is also a patron saint of poets and vegetarians. Because St David is said to have lived on a strict diet of bread, salt, water and leeks, this may be the origin of the vegetable's status as a national symbol of the Welsh.

St Aidan

Today St Aidan is best known as the first bishop and then the abbot of the important early Christian centre of Lindisfarne during the seventh century AD. However, little detail of his life before this time is known other than that he was born in Ireland. St Aidan was one of the monks on the island of Iona but came to England in 635 AD at the request of King Oswald of Northumbria. Oswald had spent a period of exile on Iona after the kingdom of Northumbria had been taken by forces from Mercia. During his time on Iona, Oswald had become a Christian and, when he returned to England, he granted St Aidan the small island of Lindisfarne as a base for converting the local population. The area of what is now north-east England and south-east Scotland was known as Bernicia and was to be the focus of St Aidan's evangelical work. He gained a reputation for renouncing worldly goods, living an austere life of poverty and devoting himself to prayer and charitable acts. St Aidan died on 31 August 651 AD at Bamburgh. He was buried on Lindisfarne in the church cemetery but the bones of the saint were moved into the church itself at a later date.

St Chad

St Chad and his brother St Cedd lived during the seventh century AD and were born in Northumbria. They both received their training at Lindisfarne with St Aidan. St Chad was sent to Ireland by St Aidan where he worked with St Egbert. He was later chosen by King Oswin or Osiu of Northumbria to be the bishop of York although the king's son Alcfrith had actually promised the see to St Wilfred who had travelled to France to be consecrated by St Agilbert. St Chad, by contrast, was ordained in England by Bishop Wine of Dorchester. In 669 AD St Chad was removed from office by St Theodore of Canterbury because he objected to St Chad's ordination by Bishop Wine, a churchman whom the Venerable Bede describes as keeping Easter in contravention of accepted canonical custom. However, St Theodore was later so impressed by St Chad's humility and holiness that he reconsecrated him and appointed him Bishop of Mercia. St Chad made the seat of his diocese in Lichfield where he established a monastery. Although St Chad was to serve for only around three years before his death in 672 AD, his work was widely praised. He is a particularly important saint in the Midlands where over thirty churches, including St Chad's in Shrewsbury, were named in his honour as well as a number of sacred wells. His feast day is celebrated on 2 March.

The Venerable Bede

One of the most important early histories of the English Church was written by a Benedictine monk, famous today as the Venerable Bede, who is thought to have been born in about

672 AD. What is known of Bede is recorded in his most famous work *Historia Ecclesiastica Gentis Anglorum* or 'The
Ecclesiastical History of the English People'. He gives a brief
biographical description of his life in which he relates that he
was sent to join the monastery of St Peter at Monkwearmouth
in Northumbria when he was seven years old. He goes on to
say that he became a deacon at the age of nineteen and, after
training, became a priest. He also said that he became a priest
when he was thirty. Bede served under and was trained by
Abbot Benedict Biscop and Abbot Ceolfrid. It is likely that
Bede joined the monastery of Jarrow with Abbot Ceolfrid in
682 AD.

It is interesting to note that the title of the 'Venerable'
Bede may actually derive from a mistaken translation of words
on the monk's tomb at Durham Cathedral. An inscription
written in Latin on his tomb reads, 'Here lie the venerable
bones of Bede'. However, it is thought that this was wrongly
interpreted as saying, 'Here lie the bones of the Venerable
Bede'!

Lindisfarne

One of the most infamous events to take place in the history
of Lindisfarne, and one that would have dramatic repercussions for Christianity in England, was a fierce attack on the
monastic community there by a Viking raiding party. The
entry for the year 793 AD in the Anglo-Saxon Chronicles, a
collection of manuscripts charting the history of England during this period, makes for particularly compelling reading and
describes the circumstances surrounding the attack in vivid
detail as presaging a kind of cosmic disaster:

In this year fierce, foreboding omens came over the land of Northumbria, and wretchedly terrified the people. There were excessive whirlwinds, lightning storms, and fiery dragons were seen flying in the sky. These signs were followed by great famine, and shortly after in the same year, on January 8th, the ravaging of heathen men destroyed God's church at Lindisfarne through brutal robbery and slaughter: and Sicga died on February 2nd. (*The Anglo-Saxon Chronicles*, Anne Savage, p.73)

St Swithun

St Swithun is a well-known English saint who became Bishop of Winchester in 852 AD. According to legend he is said to have liked the rain and asked to be buried in the churchyard at Winchester so that it would fall on his grave. On 15 July 971 AD, the relics of St Swithun were moved into Winchester Cathedral. On the day of the translation of his bones it was observed that a number of people were cured of their ills and these extraordinary events were attributed to the intercessory power of St Swithun. Most famously, on the day of the translation of his relics there was extremely heavy rainfall and this phenomenon too was believed to have been caused by the powers of the saint. A tradition has persisted right up to the present day that, if it rains upon St Swithun's Day, then it will rain for the next forty days.

St Dunstan

One major consequence of the constant raids and attacks made by the Vikings against England in the centuries before the Norman Conquest was the dramatic disruption of monastic life. St Dunstan is regarded as a pivotal figure in restoring these traditions and re-invigorating the English Church. He was born in 909 AD at Baltonsborough, close to Glastonbury in Somerset. St Dunstan came from an important family and was sent to Glastonbury to be schooled. At the time the abbey at Glastonbury was in ruins and he received his education there from Irish monks. His father was a Wessex nobleman called Heorstan and his mother Cynethryth was said to have been a devoted Christian. His uncle Athelm was an even more significant figure who was made Archbishop of Canterbury in 914. St Dunstan developed a reputation as a keen student with an aptitude for artistic and academic pursuits.

He served at St Mary's church in Glastonbury before becoming a member of Athelm's household at the request of his uncle. His success there led to him being called to join the court of King Athelstan. However, in 935 AD, his service at King Athelstan's court came to an abrupt end when he was accused of being a magician who studied witchcraft and the occult. It is curious to note that the charges made against him were that he had been 'studying the vain poems and futile stories of the pagans'. (*Oxford Dictionary of Saints*, David Farmer, p.152) Some have speculated that he was the victim of jealousy at court but it seems likely that his love of study simply drew him to look outside the narrow confines of learning imposed upon him. He subsequently travelled to Winchester where he took monastic vows under Elphege, Bishop of Winchester. St Dunstan then returned to Glastonbury where he lived as a hermit and devoted himself to the pursuit of the arts and crafts, practising and perfecting such skills as writing, painting, metalwork and playing the harp. He is thought to have included a small self-portrait of himself in an Anglo-Saxon illuminated manuscript called the 'Glastonbury Classbook' and his renown as an artist and craftsman grew during his time as a hermit at Glastonbury.

After his difficulties at the court of King Athelstan his fortunes changed. He became an advisor to the king's niece who left money to him when she died. He also grew financially richer when his own father died and, when Edmund was crowned king of Wessex, he was summoned to his court. Once again St Dunstan became the focus of court intrigues but, when King Edmund was nearly killed during a hunting accident, his fortunes changed again. According to accounts of the time, Edmund was nearly carried over a cliff by his horse but, at that exact moment, was said to have thought of St Dunstan's poor treatment at his court and promised to rectify the situation if he survived the imminent disaster. Miraculously, his horse is said to have stopped in its tracks and the king's life was saved. In thanks, Edmund made St Dunstan the abbot of Glastonbury and gave him money to rebuild and extend the abbey and its buildings. St Dunstan reversed the decline of the abbey at Glastonbury and its monks adopted the Benedictine rule.

In 946 AD, King Edmund was assassinated and succeeded by King Edred to whom St Dunstan was such a loyal servant and advisor that the king entrusted him with part of the royal treasure. However, upon his death, St Dunstan found himself at odds with his successor King Edwy and was once again driven from court. This time, fearing for his life, he fled to the Abbey of Mont Blandin near Ghent in Flanders. His stay at the abbey was to be of great importance because it gave him the opportunity to see at first hand a monastery that followed strict observance to the Benedictine rule and had undergone a reformation of organisation. When King Edgar took the throne in 957 AD, St Dunstan was appointed Bishop of Worcester. Two years later he became Bishop of London and then rose to the rank of Archbishop of Canterbury the following year. The strong relationship between King Edgar and St Dunstan allowed for new and dramatic reforms within the English Church. St Dunstan implemented monastic rules which demanded that monks lead pious and dedicated lives and succeeded, to some extent, in ending corruption within the Church such as the practice of simony or selling church positions for money. He also made celibacy an important feature of monastic life. A strong and clear link was made between the monasteries and the king, which largely freed them from the power of local lords. By the same token, the kingdom as a whole saw a greater degree of coherent organisation and unification. For example, the king assembled a navy to protect the land from Viking raids and units were formed with the express purpose of repelling any such attacks in the north of England.

In retrospect, and particularly in the period following the Norman invasion, this phase of English life came to be seen as a time of great peace and prosperity, characterised by the maintenance of high standards of law and order. St Dunstan was such an important figure within English society that he had the king put off his own coronation. He waited a full fourteen years before being officially crowned king. This may have been as some form of penance or punishment imposed by St Dunstan. When the coronation took place in 973 AD, it was performed by St Dunstan who had planned the ceremony himself. It was envisaged as a high point in the king's reign and other powerful rulers of the time, including kings from Scotland, recognised Edgar as effectively the High King.

Elements of the ceremony that St Dunstan had created have survived to the present day and form part of the modern British coronation ceremony. Although St Dunstan continued to have an active role in state life through the reigns of Edgar's successors, Edward and Ethelred the Unready, he withdrew increasingly into monastic life at Canterbury as he grew older. He died at the age of seventy-nine on 19 May 988 AD.

Following his death, he was recognised as a saint and his cult amongst the English was extremely popular. He was buried at Canterbury Cathedral which was burnt down in 1074 AD. When the new cathedral was built his remains were translated to the new building. However, Glastonbury Abbey also claimed to be the resting place of the relics of St Dunstan, a claim that was eventually dismissed in 1508 when his tomb within Canterbury Cathedral was opened and his relics were found to be intact.

Today, it is recognised that he played an important role in shaping early English history and traditions. Because of his own skill and work in the arts and crafts, he is the patron saint of goldsmiths, locksmiths and jewellers. In religious art St Dunstan is often shown with a pair of tongs. This is because of a story that the devil once tried to tempt the saint who then held him by the nose with a pair of tongs. Another interesting myth regarding the saint is claimed by some to be the basis of the belief in lucky horseshoes. According to tradition, the devil once asked St Dunstan to re-shoe his horse. St Dunstan is said to have then nailed the shoe to the devil's own hoof. When the devil cried in pain, the saint said that he would take it off if the devil agreed that he would never enter a house with a horseshoe placed over the door.

Saints and Other World Religions

Whilst the concept of sainthood is essentially a Christian one, it is clear that many other world religions view certain individuals as in some way sacred or holy.

It is interesting to note how many parallels exist between apparently different cultures and observe the ways in which different religions with common roots have intertwining features. This is clearly demonstrated by the fact that certain figures and individuals, amongst them a number of Christian saints, have come to be revered by a number of different religions and faith systems.

Angel Gabriel

The Archangel Gabriel is of great significance within the Abrahamic religions of Christianity, Judaism and Islam. Gabriel is consistently envisioned as God's messenger and his name means 'man of God'. He is conceived of as being second only in importance within the Heavenly Host to the Archangel Michael.

In the Old Testament the Archangel Gabriel helps Daniel to interpret his visions (Daniel 8: 15 and 9: 21). In the New Testament, Gabriel appears to the aged Zechariah and tells him that his wife will give birth to the prophet St John the

Baptist (Luke 1: 11–20). Most importantly for Christians it is Gabriel who is the messenger that tells Mary that she will give birth to Jesus (Luke 1: 26–38). However, for Muslims, Gabriel is also hugely important because it is Gabriel who appeared to Mohammed in 610 AD in a cave near Mecca and who instructed him to recite a number of verses that had been sent by God. During the course of his life, Mohammed continued to receive these verses and, after his death, they were written down and given the title of the 'Quran'. In fact, the very meaning of the word Quran is recitation. Muslims refer to Gabriel as Gibrail.

Because of his biblical role as a divine messenger he has in recent years come to be seen as the patron saint of occupations that relate to communications of any kind. In 1951, Pope Pius XII officially decreed that the Archangel Gabriel was patron saint of the telecommunications industries, including television workers and telephonists. His patronage also extends to postal workers and diplomats and even stamp collectors. Perhaps unsurprisingly, given the importance of Gabriel's role in announcing the birth of Jesus, he is also viewed as a patron saint of childbirth.

Although Gabriel is described as a saint, he is not imagined as a mortal soul in heaven. Use of 'saint' in referring to him simply denotes that he is viewed as 'holy' in the original sense of the word 'saint'. Traditionally the feast of the Archangel Gabriel was celebrated on 24 March in the Western Church. The Annunciation of Mary is celebrated on 25 March. In the Eastern Church the feast of the Archangel Gabriel is held on 26 March. However, since 1969, his feast has been combined with that of the Archangel Michael and All Angels on 29 September. This feast also includes the Archangel Raphael. Raphael appears in the Old Testament in the Books of Enoch and Tobit and his role is to bring the prayers of the faithful before God. His name is said to mean 'God Heals'.

St John the Baptist

The figure of St John the Baptist is revered in both Christianity and Islam as well as by a number of other religious groups, including the Mandaeans. Within Christianity St John the Baptist is of great importance because he is the prophet in the New Testament who announces the coming of Christ. In the Old Testament his life and work is foretold by the prophet Isaiah who says that:

> A voice cries out: 'In the wilderness prepare the way of the Lord, make straight in the desert a highway for our God'. (Isaiah 40:3).

Luke relates that Mary, the mother of Jesus, was a relative of Elizabeth, the mother of St John the Baptist. In religious art, St John the Baptist is depicted with long wild hair and beard and is dressed in clothes made from animal skins. In some traditions he is clad in a single camel skin and is described in the Bible as living and preaching in the desert. He is said to have lived a pious and holy life, disdaining worldly goods and comforts and living on a diet of locusts and honey.

St John the Baptist's outspoken criticisms of King Herod led to his capture and arrest. Herod had married his brother's wife and St John the Baptist declared this to be unlawful. However, Herod was impressed by the saint. He regarded him as a holy man and, although he kept him imprisoned, he admired him. But his wife Herodias conspired to cause his death and tricked Herod into executing him. When her daughter

Salome danced for Herod and his guests at a banquet, the king was so impressed that he offered her anything that she wanted as a reward. Herodias seized her chance and instructed Salome to ask for the head of St John the Baptist on a plate. The date celebrated as the day of the saint's martyrdom is 29 August.

As previously mentioned, St John the Baptist is also a significant figure within other religions. For the Mandaeans, who refer to him as Yaha, he is seen as the last and most important prophet. Members of the Baha'i faith believe that an important figure within their movement was actually St John the Baptist returned to the world. He is referred to as Yahya in the Quran and, as in Christian teachings, he is said to be the son of the priest Zechariah. He is described as the cousin of Jesus Christ and is similarly seen as a great prophet.

During the Middle Ages the saint became extremely popular and many churches were named in his honour. Interestingly, a number of churches built in wild woodland areas within the English county of Shropshire, such as St John's Church at Kenley, were dedicated in his honour because of his reputation for preaching in the wilderness. He was also the patron saint of the military order of the Knights Hospitaller who are also known as the Knights of St John of Rhodes and Malta. The original purpose of the order was to protect pilgrims who had travelled to the Holy Land and to care for the sick in the hospital that they founded in Jerusalem in the latter half of the eleventh century. According to the chronicler William of Tyre the founders of the order, who were merchants from Amalfi, dedicated the hospital to St John the Almoner. However, it is now thought that, writing about a century after the event, he was mistaken in this belief. It is now generally accepted that it was dedicated to St John the

Baptist and this idea is supported by the fact that the cathedral at Amalfi was dedicated to the Virgin Mary and St John the Baptist.

In more recent years the author Keith Laidler, in his book *The Head of God*, and other writers have speculated that the legendary military order of the Knights Templar may have been part of what is termed as the Johannite Heresy. Some religious groups believed that John the Baptist was not simply the prophet of the coming of Jesus Christ, but was himself the messiah. Fuel for this speculation was the accusation levelled at the Templars, during the trial for heresy that led to their dissolution, that they had worshipped various sacred heads in their rituals and ceremonies. It has recently been suggested that a number of the round churches built by the Knights Templar during the Middle Ages, which have a design supposedly based on the Church of the Holy Sepulchre in Jerusalem, are in fact aligned to the point of sunrise on the morning of the feast day of the saint to whom the church has been dedicated. It has also been suggested that the famous London Temple may be aligned to the position in which the sun rises on 29 August, the feast day of the death of St John the Baptist who was an important and much venerated saint within the order. Another example of the remains of a Templar church that apparently corresponds to this particular alignment can be found at Dover.

The Ummayad Mosque

The shrine of St John the Baptist is today located in the Ummayad Mosque, also known as the Grand Mosque of Damascus in Syria. It is a fascinating example of how a sacred site with ancient origins has continued to serve an important religious function for a varied number of faith groups over a very long period of time. The earliest known use of this site for religious purposes dates from the Aramean period when a temple of Hadad was built there. During the pre-Christian Roman period it became the site of a temple dedicated to Jupiter. Its function was to change again in the Byzantine era when Christianity was the dominant religion of the Eastern Roman Empire and a church was built there, importantly one that was dedicated to St John the Baptist.

Following the loss of Damascus to Muslim forces in 636 AD, during the reign of the Byzantine emperor Heraclius, the church built on the site was left unharmed. In fact, it was jointly used by Christians and Muslims, although eventually an extension made of mud brick was erected against the south wall of the church where Muslims could pray. This situation continued until around 706 AD when, under the rule of the Caliph Al-Walid I of the Umayyad dynasty, it was destroyed and the mosque that exists today was built in its place. It is said that the Caliph symbolically began the task of taking down the church by striking it with a golden spike. When preparations were being made for the building of the mosque, a team of workmen supposedly discovered the head of St John the Baptist. Following this great discovery, a shrine was subsequently built to house this most precious religious relic.

Interestingly, Caliph Al-Walid I was aided in building the mosque by the Byzantine Emperor Justinian II who despatched a skilled team of craftsmen, large quantities of gold and materials such as mosaic tesserae to him for the purpose. Like many other mosques (and Islamic architecture in general) it consequently displays strong Byzantine influence. The Ummayad Mosque was intended for a number of functions, not only incorporating religious activities but also serving as a site for the dispensation of law. It was intended to reflect the design of the house of the Prophet Muhammad in Medina which had also combined religious and social purposes. At the time, it was one of the largest buildings in the world and its interior is similar to that of the Dome of the Rock in Jerusalem. It also contained the largest golden mosaic in existence. The Ummayad Mosque is also significant in that it was the first mosque to have a prayer hall which contained three aisles that allowed worshippers to view the *mihrab*. This is an alcove that indicates to Muslims the way they must pray in order to be facing Mecca, the most significant religious site in the Islamic world. In addition, the Ummayad Mosque is notable for containing the tomb of the legendary Muslim leader Saladin. Reflecting the importance of the figure of St John the Baptist to Muslims and Christians alike, Pope John Paul II visited his shrine at the Ummayad Mosque in 2001.

However, the Ummayad Mosque is not the only shrine to claim to hold the surviving relics of St John the Baptist. According to a number of historians from the ancient world including Nicephorus, Josephus and Symeon Metaphrastes, King Herod ordered that the head of the saint be buried at Machaerus within the fortress. Probably the earliest place to be associated with holding his remains is a shrine at Sebaste in Samaria. According to the Roman historian Rufinus, the shrine was attacked by the pagan emperor Julian the Apostate in 362 AD. Apparently the saint's bones were burned but some of his remains were retrieved. They were then taken to Alexandria in Egypt and placed in a basilica on 27 May 395 AD. As is the case with many other saints, there are numerous locations that claim to hold some portion of John's relics, including Amiens Cathedral in France and San Silvestro in Capite in the city of Rome.

Elijah

The prophet Elijah offers a fascinating example of how Jewish, Christian and Islamic traditions and mythologies are interlinked and interwoven. Elijah lived during the ninth century BC and is an important figure within the Christian Bible, the Quran and the Talmud. In Jewish tradition the return of Elijah to the earth will announce the coming of the messiah. He is of particular interest within this context because, in the New Testament, it was thought that St John the Baptist might, in fact, be Elijah.

In the Gospel of Luke, an angel of the Lord appears to the priest Zechariah in the temple and announces that his wife Elizabeth will bear him a son who will be called John. The child will be the prophet John the Baptist and the angel tells Zechariah that, 'He will turn many of the people of Israel to the Lord their God. With the spirit and power of Elijah he will go before them, to turn the hearts of parents to their children, and the disobedient to the wisdom of the righteous, to make ready a people prepared for the Lord.' (Luke 1:16–17)

Both prophets shared similar characteristics – preaching in the wilderness, declaring that judgement day was approaching – and both taught the importance of worshipping the God of the Israelites. Indeed, following preaching the coming of the Son of God, St John the Baptist was summoned to speak to the Pharisees. 'This is the testimony given by John when the Jews sent priests and Levites from Jerusalem to ask him, "Who are you?" He confessed and did not deny it, but confessed, "I am not the Messiah." And they asked him, "What then? Are you Elijah?" He said, "I am not."' (John 1:21)

Interestingly, the prophet Elijah has also been identified

with the figure of St George whose tomb at Lydda, or modern day Lod in Palestine, is a focus of worship for Christians, Muslims and Jews. Today the shrine of St George is located within an Eastern Orthodox church next to a mosque. In Islamic tradition, St George is identified with the figure of Al Khidr whose name means 'the Green One'. It is thought that elements of the life of the prophet Elijah have influenced and become interwoven with stories and legends relating to both St George and Al Khidr.

There are also parallels between saints in the Christian sense and those individuals who are referred to as the tzadikim within Judaism. Those who are deemed to be particularly worthy or righteous are described as a tzadik. This Hebrew word translates as 'righteous one' although other traditions also claim that a tzadik is an individual who does not commit sins and furthermore is not tempted or interested in sinning. According to the Talmud, there are always thirty-six tzadiks alive in the world. It also states dramatically that it is only because of the existence of these unique sinless individuals that the world continues to exist. It is also believed that such particularly holy figures can, through prayer, achieve miracles.

Sufism

Sufism has been defined as a kind of mystical tradition within the religion of Islam. It is a tradition that is thought to have developed during the eighth century AD and has been described as offering a path towards the Divine and, in this sense, has been referred to as the 'Sufi Way'. It has been observed that the reverence held for a number of figures within Sufism has elements that are comparable to the Christian veneration of saints. Chief amongst these is the practice of turning the graves or tombs of the individuals who are believed to have been figures of great holiness or piety into shrines where the anniversary of their deaths is observed as a form of feast in much the same way as saints' days are celebrated within Christianity. Many Sufi saints are also claimed to have performed miracles in their lifetimes or it is claimed that miracles took place at their shrines after their deaths.

The tomb of Abda al-Qadir al-Jilani in Baghdad is one of the most important Sufi shrines and he is thought to have the power to act as an intercessor or mediator between Muslims and the Divine. He was born in Persia in around 1077 AD and is believed to be the founder of the Qadiriyah order. This order is part of the tradition of Sufism. He emerged as an important preacher in around 1127 and he is credited with achieving a harmonious balance between Sufi mysticism and sterner aspects of Muslim society such as its justice system. As with many Christian saints his biographical details have become intertwined with legend and myth. Like many other Sufis, the Muslim Sufi saint Sultan Bahu, who lived from 1628 to 1691, referred to Abda al-Qadir al-Jilani as his spiritual master. Sultan Bahu was part of the Qadiriyah Sufi Order that he had formed and went on to form a new but related order of Sufism called Sarwari Qadiri. Many Sufi saints were hugely productive writers and Sultan Bahu is said to have written as many as forty books about Sufism. He is particularly popular in the Punjab region of Pakistan where he was born and his poetry is sung by Sufis in the area today. His shrine is at Garh Maharaja in Pakistan and a lively and popular annual festival is held there.

It is also interesting to note that the concept of a patron saint of a particular place is not simply confined to Christian traditions and is also familiar in Islam. The great grandson of the Prophet Muhammad himself, Abdullah Shah Ghazi, is regarded as being the patron saint of Karachi in Pakistan. Because he was a descendant of the prophet and a member of the tribe of Banu Hashim, his popularity was said to have created rivalry with the Ummayad dynasty. There was considerable enmity between these two groups and an Ummayad army was sent to Pakistan to kill Abdullah Shah Ghazi. It is said that the army came upon him whilst he was hunting and that, rather than be captured or give into the aggressors, he bravely chose to stay and fight.

His bravery in the face of a huge army earned him the appellation 'Ghazi' that translates as him having been 'victorious'. The shrine of Abdullah Shah Ghazi in Karachi is hugely popular and, as with the shrines of many Western saints, it is believed that miracles have taken place there and that devotees may ask for a wish to be granted. His anniversary is celebrated with a festival held over the course of three days.

Hinduism

It has also been observed that there are sacred or holy figures within Hinduism who hold a similar religious significance to the one saints do within Christianity. However, it must be emphasised that within Hinduism there is no institutional process leading to canonisation. Instead, as in the early Christian Church, this is more of a process of popular acclamation and local recognition. There are a number of comparable phrases used within Hinduism to denote the sanctity or saintliness of an individual. They can include 'mahatma' and 'paramahamsa' and also 'swami'. Individuals who are recognised in this way are also commonly referred to as 'Sri' or 'Srila' in a similar if not identical way to the Christian term of 'St'. In northern India there is a tradition of naming individuals who are regarded as holy as 'sant', which seems astonishingly close to the Western term of 'saint'. The term 'sant' is, in fact, derived from the Sanskrit word for 'truth' or 'reality'. It can also mean a person who has a mystical understanding of truth or reality.

Perhaps the most famous individual to be named as a mahatma in the modern era is, of course, Mohandas K Ghandi whose philosophy of non-violent action led to Indian independence from British colonial rule. Historically, there is a wide number of such notable individuals within Hinduism such as Chaitanya Mahaprabhu who was born in 1486 in Bengal. He was a Vaishnava monk and an important advocate of 'Bhakti' yoga. This translates as a 'loving devotion to Krishna'. He is best known today as having been the founder of the religious group known as the Hare Krishna sect.

The Indian guru Shirdi Sai Baba, who was born in 1838, is of particular interest in this context because he is regarded as being a saint-like figure by both Hindus and Muslims. Perhaps unsurprisingly, Buddhists also have a comparable saint tradition and have a particular regard for individuals they term as the Arhats.

Saints in the Middle Ages

In many ways the veneration of saints reached an apogee during the Middle Ages when their help and influence were sought at all levels of society and formed an integral part of daily life. A major development in the nature of sainthood was the assertion of the right of the papacy to canonise certain individuals. This increasing level of control of religious matters reflected the growing powers of the Roman Catholic Church and the right to canonise was formalised under Innocent III, who was pope from 1199 to 1216. Another major influence on the development of the cult of saints was the effect of the religious wars in the Middle East generally referred to as the crusades. Many Eastern Christian saints gained popularity in the west during this period, although it could be argued that their original identities often became obscured in the process.

St Francis of Assisi

Today St Francis of Assisi appears to enjoy an almost unique popularity amongst saints that seemingly reaches beyond the confines of the Christian faith. In the popular imagination St Francis is closely linked to a respect for, and appreciation of, the natural world that is shared by many. However, some have argued that this aspect of the life and mythology of St Francis has been overemphasised and does not accurately reflect his teachings and beliefs. St Francis was the son of a successful and wealthy cloth merchant in Assisi called Pietro di Bernardone. He was born on 26 September 1181 when his father was away from home and working in France. His mother Pica Bourlemont was French and came from Provence. She is said to have had ambitions for her son to become an important figure within the Church and originally had him baptised as John after St John the Baptist. When his father returned from France, he insisted that he be renamed Francesco, meaning 'the Frenchman'. This apparently was to acknowledge his mother's nationality and Pietro's absence in France at the time of his birth.

Although his father was keen for him to join his business, St Francis showed little interest and reputedly spent much time reading as a young man. Early in life he gained a reputation for having a disdain for riches, giving away his money to beggars, much to his father's annoyance. His friends were also the sons of wealthy businessmen and the nobility and, in 1201, he took part in fighting between his hometown of Assisi and Perugia. He was captured by the Perugians and spent a year as a prisoner. He became ill and returned to Assisi in 1203. Following the fighting, he is said to have followed an increasingly spiritual path, helping to nurse lepers and begging for the poor.

St Francis claimed to have undergone a crucial turning point in his life when visiting the dilapidated Church of San Damiano of Assisi. Whilst he was regarding a crucifix within the church it appeared to him that the Byzantine icon of Christ on the cross spoke to him, saying:

Francis, go and repair my house, which you see is falling down.

St Francis believed that he had been instructed to repair the damaged church and sold some of his father's cloth to raise money for the work. This greatly angered his father and the conflict between the two reached a head when St Francis renounced all his worldly goods, including his substantial inheritance, in front of the Bishop of Assisi. He even abandoned the clothes that his father had given him and was given a humbler outfit in their stead by the bishop.

St Francis chose to embrace what he termed as 'Lady Poverty' in his new life devoted to God. He restored the Church of San Damiano by appealing to the rich of Assisi and he lived as a beggar. He was said to have also been inspired by Christ's words to his disciples in Matthew 10:9 in which he tells them to preach the arrival of the Kingdom of Heaven. They are told to travel without money or comforts and St Francis decided to follow their example, travelling as a beggar and preaching. His sermons drew admiration and he was soon joined by a small number of disciples of his own. They set up a small religious community at a small chapel close to Assisi called the Portiuncula, dedicated to St Mary of the Angels. In 1209, St Francis decided to approach the papacy to grant him the right to begin a new religious order of brothers. Legend tells that Pope Innocent III first denied St Francis an audience but, after Innocent had a dream in which he saw a crumbling church being supported by St Francis, he decided to authorise the foundation of the Franciscan Order.

One aspect of the life and teachings of St Francis that is perhaps not always recognised is that he was a strict follower of Roman Catholic orthodoxy and dogma in religious matters. The rule of the order laid out by St Francis in a work entitled *Regula Prima* was officially recognised by the pope in

1210. The Franciscan brothers lived simple austere lives without great wealth, fine buildings or comforts.

St Francis became a popular figure in Italy through his sermons but soon he was no longer content simply to preach in his own country. In 1211, St Francis boarded a ship to travel to Jerusalem but the journey ended in disaster when he was shipwrecked on the coast of Dalmatia. Three years later, another attempt to preach abroad failed when he became very ill en route to Morocco. He was forced to return to Italy. However, in 1219, St Francis and twelve friars sailed for the Holy Land. Upon arrival he was greatly disappointed by the behaviour and attitude of the crusader soldiers that he met. Incredibly, he decided to travel from the safety of the Christian-held territories to meet Sultan Melek-el-Kamel in an attempt to convert him and his followers to Christianity. The sultan is said to have received him with courtesy and was impressed by the sermons of St Francis. However, they failed to convert the sultan and St Francis returned to the lands held by the Christians.

One of the most important events in the life of St Francis occurred whilst he was praying on Mount La Verna in 1224. He undertook a period of fasting that lasted for forty days and was intended to be a preparation for celebrating Michaelmas. He is said to have experienced a vision on 14 September and dramatically underwent the Impression of the Stigmata. During this experience he manifested the five wounds that Christ received on the cross when nails were driven through his hands and feet and his side was pierced by the spear of the Roman legionary Longinus. This is thought to be the earliest authentic account of an individual displaying stigmata, a phenomenon considered, particularly within the Roman Catholic Church, to be an indication of the holiness of the individual who experiences it and one that should be counted a great privilege and a miracle.

It is interesting to note that the best-known stories linked to the life of St Francis are primarily derived from posthumous folklore and myths. Many are recounted in the collection of tales about St Francis called the 'Fioretti' or the 'little flowers'. They detail his great love of the natural world, the environment and the creatures that live within it. Most famously, of course, St Francis is said to have preached to the birds, creating an image that has been a popular subject for many artists over the centuries since his death. He is said to have been on a journey with a small group of friends when they noticed a number of trees filled with birds that were singing loudly. According to the legend the saint told those who accompanied him that he was going to preach to his 'sisters the birds'. The birds were said to be drawn by the sermon that he gave and listened intently to him. He told them that God loved and blessed them and that they, like people, should seek always to praise God.

According to the Fioretti, St Francis also once miraculously tamed a wolf that was terrorising the city of Gubbio. It had been eating their livestock and had even killed people from the city. St Francis decided to resolve this difficult situation and went to find it in the nearby hills. It is said that when St Francis came across the wolf he had a miraculous power over it and ordered it to lie still before him. Instead of killing it or banishing it, the saint was said to have showed compassion and pity and recognised that the wolf had killed because it was hungry. Therefore he took the wolf back to the city and asked the people to feed the animal regularly. In return for this the wolf would no longer attack them or their livestock. A well-known piece of writing by St Francis is the 'Canticle of the Sun' in which he praises the natural world around him. He refers to the 'Brother Sun' and the 'Sister Moon' and also, perhaps most resonantly for readers in recent years, 'Mother Earth'.

St Thomas Becket

St Thomas Becket was undoubtedly one of the most important and popular English saints of the Middle Ages. His life was dramatic and turbulent and he was a hugely controversial figure in the society in which he lived but he was (and is) revered as a martyr who died defending his faith. He was born in 1118 at Cheapside in the city of London. His parents were Gilbert of Thiereville, Normandy and Matilda who was from Caen. They were wealthy and, as a youth, he received a good education.

He was educated at Merton Priory in England from the age of ten and was later taken on by Theobald, Archbishop of Canterbury, who sent him to Auxerre and Bologna for further study. After performing a number of important missions on behalf of the archbishop in Rome, he was appointed archdeacon of Canterbury in 1154. He also became Provost of Beverley. In the same year, Henry II became King of England and, on Theobald's recommendation, appointed Becket as his Chancellor.

At first the relationship between Henry II and St Thomas seemed to be an excellent and fruitful one, and the English king appeared well pleased with the Chancellor's successes in his diplomatic and political duties. In 1162, Henry took steps to promote his Chancellor to the post of Archbishop of Canterbury. In this new role Becket took what he felt to be his responsibilities extremely seriously and chose a lifestyle of austerity and piety that was in many ways at odds with his behaviour as Chancellor. He is often portrayed in medieval sources as wearing a hair shirt beneath the rich robes to which his position entitled him and as living a virtuous and secretly austere life. Becket and Henry II became such close friends that the king even sent his own son, also named Henry, to live within the archbishop's household. It was common at this time for nobles to send their children to grow up in the houses of their wealthy, important contemporaries.

However, the intention of Henry II in installing his friend and ally Becket in the position of archbishop was so that he could exert greater control over the English Church. Becket, who had different ideas, turned away from his role as Chancellor and focussed instead on the duties of his position as Archbishop of Canterbury. He also took control of the revenue created by the holdings that the archbishopric of Canterbury held, increasing his own personal power. Becket and the king came into conflict in the courts when Henry II attempted to increase his powers at the expense of the Church and the archbishop refused to yield ground. On 30 January 1164, King Henry II convened an assembly at Clarendon Palace with the aim of reducing the power and rights of the Church and distancing the English clergy from the papacy. Although Henry II managed to persuade the assembly to agree to his new constitutions, Becket would not add his signature to the papers. The refusal by the archbishop to accede to the king's wishes led Henry II to order Becket to appear at a court in Northampton in 1164 to be charged with failing to recognise the authority of the king. Becket fled to seek the protection of Louis VII of France and, for two years, he was given shelter at the abbey at Pontigny.

Whilst in exile Becket approached Pope Alexander III for assistance in his conflict with the king. The pope attempted to resolve the differences between the two through dialogue and was initially unwilling to take the extreme measure of excommunication against Henry. However, under pressure from Becket, Alexander III eventually came to consider this ultimate sanction seriously and Henry II relented, offering to reach some sort of agreement with the archbishop. Becket returned to Canterbury in 1170 but was soon in conflict with the king once again, this time over the crowning of Prince Henry without his involvement or consent. Angered by the failure of the king to recognise his role as head of the Church in England, Becket excommunicated the bishops who had carried out the ceremony. It was at this point that the king is famously said to have shouted in a rage to his courtiers, 'Will no one rid me of this turbulent priest?' So dramatic were the remonstrations of the king that four knights from his court decided to carry out what they believed were their sovereign's wishes. The four men were Hugh de Moreville, Reginald Fitzurse, Richard le Breton and William de Tracey. They confronted Becket on Tuesday 29 December 1170 inside Canterbury Cathedral and, after an argument, they attacked and killed him.

As he was attacked by the knights, he is said to have been steadfast in his faith and, according to an account from the time by a witness called Edward Grim, his final words were, 'For the name of Jesus and the protection of the church, I am ready to embrace death'. Whilst many had criticised Becket for his actions as archbishop the news and the nature of his death – murdered in his own cathedral – sent shockwaves throughout the Christian world. Opinions about Becket were also altered in the aftermath of his murder by the revelation that he had worn a hair shirt under his clothes during his life.

He was viewed as a martyr for his faith and miracles were said to have taken place at his tomb. The king undertook public penance for his role in the murder and, in 1173, Becket was canonised by Pope Alexander. The tomb of Thomas Becket was to become one of the most important English sites of pilgrimage for Christians. Geoffrey Chaucer famously recorded the importance of the Pilgrims' Way from London to Canterbury in *The Canterbury Tales* and it had great religious significance beyond the confines of Britain. Becket's relics were later translated to the Trinity Chapel in 1220. He is venerated today in the Roman Catholic Church and the Church of England and his feast day is 29 December, the date of his murder.

St Michael

St Michael is the archangel who is named in the Book of Revelation as the leader or one of the chief princes of the forces of God who battle Satan. This particularly vivid episode in the Bible was to prove an immense inspiration for many artists and writers and has shaped the way in which St Michael is most commonly portrayed. It describes the conflict in powerful and dramatic terms:

And war broke out in heaven: Michael and his angels fought against the dragon. The dragon and his angels fought back, but they were defeated, and there was no longer any place for them in heaven. The great dragon was thrown down, that ancient serpent, who is called the Devil and Satan, the deceiver of the whole world, he was thrown down to the earth, and his angels were thrown down with him. (Book of Revelation 12:7–9)

He appears in the Book of Daniel where he is described as being the guardian angel who will protect the Israelites. The name Michael means 'who is like unto God' but, although he carries the title of saint, he is not believed by Christians or Jews to be a mortal. He is described as a saint in the original sense of the word, meaning 'holy'. St Michael is said to have the power to rescue souls from hell and he is often depicted in religious art holding a set of scales as he weighs the souls of the dead. He is described in the Epistle of Jude as fighting the devil for the body of Moses and during the struggle bellowing: 'May the Lord rebuke you.'

The Eastern Roman Empire, later known as the Byzantine Empire, was crucial in introducing the cult of St Michael to the West. The first Christian emperor, Constantine the Great, dedicated a church close to Constantinople to St Michael and it was believed that he could help cure health problems and illness. Many depictions of St Michael produced during the Byzantine period show him wearing armour and carrying a sword identical to that of Byzantine soldiers and they have provided often highly accurate snapshots of the appearance of warriors of the period.

During the medieval centuries, the popularity of St Michael reached something of a pinnacle and he became a patron saint of knights and soldiers and orders of chivalry. The popularity of the cult of St Michael can be observed in the many place names dedicated to him. These include such famous sites as St Michael's Mount in Cornwall, Mont St Michel in Normandy and the remains of St Michael's Church that stands upon Glastonbury Tor in Somerset in England.

Other important shrines dedicated to St Michael are St Michael's Church, Liv in the Ukraine, the Monastery of Archangel Panormitis on the Greek island of Symi and Monte Sant'Angelo sul Gargano in Italy. Today, St Michael is considered in Christianity to be the patron saint of a number of occupations but, because of his role fighting Satan, he is particularly associated with the armed forces. He is the particular patron saint of paratroopers and also of police officers. His feast day is celebrated on 29 September. Today his feast day is known as St Michael and All Angels because, within the Roman Catholic Church, it is now shared with the archangels Raphael and Gabriel.

St Christopher

The popularity of St Christopher reached its peak in Europe during the Middle Ages. Like those of many other saints, his story was crystallised in the general imagination by its inclusion in *The Golden Legend* by Jacobus de Voragine. Almost nothing is known about St Christopher but it was believed that he was a third-century martyr who was killed in Asia Minor. His name is Greek for 'Christ-bearer' and is likely to be the source of the story of St Christopher. According to one legend, St Christopher was a man of great physical stature who approached a hermit one day and asked him the best way that he could serve Christ. The hermit replied that he should take up residence near a river and help travellers to cross from one side to another. One day a child asked St Christopher if he would bear him across the river and the saint replied that he would. It was said that there had been a storm and that the river had become a raging and dangerous torrent. When he was carrying him across the flooded river, the weight of the child seemed miraculously to increase and it was with great difficulty that they reached the far bank.

The child informed him that he was, in fact, Jesus Christ himself and the reason he had been so heavy was that he carried the weight of the world on his shoulders. Christ instructed St Christopher to plant his staff in the ground and told him that it would sprout leaves and bear fruit the next day as proof that he was indeed who he said he was. When St Christopher did so it grew into a palm tree. Following this miracle St Christopher took to evangelising but was martyred during the persecution of Christians by the emperor Decius. Because of his encounter with Christ, St Christopher is famously the patron saint of travellers but he was also invoked against the plague, danger by water and from tempests and also for protection from sudden deaths. For this reason pictures of St Christopher were often painted in churches on the north wall opposite the porch so that everyone could see it. It was believed that if an individual looked at an image of St Christopher he or she would not die that day.

In the Eastern Orthodox Church, he is sometimes known somewhat bizarrely as St Christopher the Dog face. According to their traditions, St Christopher was from a Berber tribe who were cannibals and were cynocephalic, meaning that they had the heads of dogs rather than humans. He was said to be a giant of a man who embraced Christianity during the reign of the emperor Decius and preached to the unconverted. He made many new converts for Christianity but was finally martyred and his body taken to Alexandria by Peter of Attalia.

The popularity of St Christopher declined during the Reformation and he was singled out for particular criticism by

Erasmus in his *Praise of Folly*. In the modern era this trend has been dramatically reversed as travel by air and car has become an increasingly important aspect of people's lives and his protection has again become commonly invoked. St Christopher medallions today are widespread in their popularity and appeal.

St George

Although St George ranks amongst the early Christian martyrs, his fame and popularity reached their peak during the Middle Ages. For many the fact that he is revered as a martyr may come as something of a surprise, since he has been absorbed into folk culture largely through the legend of his battle with the ferocious dragon. His story is a fascinating one and he has been adopted as a patron saint by many countries, including, most famously, England. According to the earliest martyrologies, St George was killed for his faith on 23 April in 303 AD at Lydda in Palestine.

Accounts of his life are variable and unreliable to such an extent that it has been argued that he never actually existed. Some claim that he was a native of Cappadocia, a region in central Turkey, which at that time was part of the Eastern Roman Empire.

He was said to have been from a prominent and noble family and had risen through the Roman military to occupy a position of some rank. Other sources suggest that he may have occupied some other position of importance within the Roman Empire but the consensus seems to be that he was figure of some social significance. He is generally depicted as a military saint, although the earliest known icon of him does not make this explicit; he is depicted wearing robes but some have argued that armour is visible beneath them. He is said to have been a Christian who refused to renounce his faith, possibly during the persecution of Christians in the reign of the emperor Diocletian.

The legend of George fighting the dragon was crystallised in the collection of the lives of the saints compiled by Jacobus de Voragine called *The Golden Legend*. According to *The Golden Legend*, St George was a native of Cappadocia and a tribune in the Roman army who one day arrived at the city of Silena in the province of Libya. Upon his arrival he discovered that the city was being terrorised by a 'pestilential dragon' whose wrath the people were assuaging by giving it sheep from their flocks. When their sheep were consumed they decided to offer it people, chosen by lot. Eventually the king's daughter herself was chosen in this way. Although the king pleaded with his people to spare her they were unrelenting and she was offered to the dragon. St George witnessed this and charged the dragon upon his horse, striking it a terrible blow with his lance. He told the princess to throw her girdle around the neck of the defeated dragon and she led it into the city.

St George finally slew the dragon on condition that the inhabitants of the city agreed to be baptised and embrace Christianity. There has been considerable speculation about the origin of this legend, some viewing it as metaphor for individual Christians standing up to a human tyrant or 'dragon' and choosing martyrdom over denying their faith. It has been widely argued that the imagery of St George as a handsome young warrior defeating an evil monster can be traced to such Greek myths as the stories of Perseus saving Andromeda or Bellerophon and the Chimera. His feast day is 23 April.

St Sebastian

St Sebastian, like St George, was said to have been a Roman soldier who died as a martyr during the persecution of Christians by the emperor Diocletian. Little is known of his life but he is reported to have enlisted in 283 AD and was a Christian who became the captain of the elite praetorian guard – the emperor's personal bodyguard. St Sebastian offered help and assistance to a number of Christian martyrs and, when this was discovered by Diocletian, he was sentenced to be shot to death with arrows. However, he survived this ordeal and appeared again before the astonished emperor who had him clubbed to death.

Although the actual martyrdom of St Sebastian was achieved through his being brutally beaten to death with clubs, it is the story of his having been shot with arrows that is most identified with his cult. It has proved to be an enormously popular subject for painters such as El Greco, Botticelli and Bernini. It has been argued that the popularity of the subject was because it gave painters the opportunity to depict a semi-naked young man in a religious context and that images of St Sebastian often have unmistakably erotic overtones. In this sense, St Sebastian has become something of a gay icon and this theme has been explored by the filmmaker Derek Jarman amongst others. The western feast day of St Sebastian is 20 January and in the Eastern Church it is celebrated on 18 December. He is a patron saint of archers, soldiers and the police and was invoked against the plague.

St Catherine

It was claimed particularly during the Middle Ages that St Catherine or Katharine of Alexandria was a Christian martyr who died for her faith during the fourth century AD. However, none of the earliest lives of the saints makes mention of her.

According to accounts of her life, St Catherine was a Christian born into a rich family from Alexandria. It is said that, in 305 AD, the emperor Maxentius seized a number of women from Alexandria, including St Catherine. In trying to convert the saint from Christianity, the emperor is said to have assembled a group of no less than fifty pagan philosophers to try to convince her to abandon her faith in Christ. Reportedly, she defeated them in this debate and went on to convert them to Christianity. In a fit of rage Maxentius ordered that the philosophers be put to death along with subsequent converts and had St Catherine imprisoned. Finally, the emperor ordered that she be executed by being tied to a wooden wheel set with spikes or blades. When the order was given to execute St Catherine the wheel to which she was fastened was mysteriously broken into pieces, leaving her unharmed. Some claimed that it had been broken by angels. She was then martyred by being beheaded. According to the accounts of her life, no blood was shed when the sword struck her neck but, bizarrely, milk and honey poured forth.

The modern term for the spinning firework called a 'catherine wheel' derives from this story. She became a particularly popular saint during the Middle Ages when the legend of her martyrdom was carried back to the West by soldiers and pilgrims returning from the crusades. For example, she was a particular favourite of the warrior monks the

Knights Templar after a military victory they achieved against Saladin at the battle of Ramleh on her feast day of 25 November in 1177. They dedicated a number of churches in her honour including that of St Catherine's at Temple on Bodmin Moor in Cornwall.

St Joan of Arc

St Joan of Arc was born in 1412 in Domrémy in the Champagne region of France. She grew up during the violence and turbulence of the Hundred Years War between England and France. At the age of fourteen, she had a series of mystical experiences when she believed that a number of voices spoke to her and set her upon an important quest. She said that St Michael, St Margaret of Antioch and St Catherine of Alexandria had all communicated with her and that their message had been that she had to set France free. Initially, she was regarded with scepticism by the French leaders but she continued with her claims and won greater favour when she foretold events surrounding the failure of the French armies that appeared to come true.

Her reputation grew to the extent that she was allowed to meet the Dauphin, later to become Charles VII. It is said that Joan of Arc distinguished herself to him by seeing through a disguise he was wearing. According to legend, she is also supposed to have shown the Dauphin some form of secret sign that convinced him that her claims were real and that she had been given some kind of divine mission.

Her claims were further tested by a group of theologians who spent three weeks questioning her and finally concluded that she was of potential use to the French in the struggle against the English. When a French force was gathered to help to lift the English siege of the city of Orleans, Joan asked that she might join them and requested that she be provided with arms. Her request was granted and it is said that she rode with the French troops wearing a white suit of armour. Although the French war leaders were reluctant to attack the enemy with any vigour, Joan insisted that they should and, within nine days, the siege was ended. It was an important event in lifting French morale and more victories followed.

In July 1429, Charles VII was crowned at Reims and Joan was present, bearing her standard. However, she was later captured at Compiègne by Burgundians who were fighting with the English. She was left in their hands by Charles VII and was tried as a heretic and a witch. Through intimidation and an unfair trial, she was found guilty and was burnt at the stake in Rouen on 30 May 1431. She was aged only nineteen when she died. In 1456, Pope Callistus III re-investigated her case and declared that she was innocent. Joan was later beatified by Pope Pius X and on 16 May 1920 she was officially canonised by Pope Benedict XV. She is a saint who has appealed to a variety of people from feminists to writers and artists and she is a symbol of patriotism and national courage in France.

Saints During the Reformation

The Protestant Reformation of the sixteenth century was to have an enormous impact on the development of Christianity and the veneration of saints. The Roman Catholic Church at this time was viewed by many Christians as corrupt and immoral, particularly in its widespread practice of selling indulgences. This involved the Church selling documents to individuals that promised forgiveness of their sins and effectively promised a reduction of the time that they would spend in purgatory. This activity, together with simony or the selling of positions within the Church, horrified many Christians who believed that the Church had truly lost its way. Most prominent amongst these dissenting voices was that of Martin Luther who famously nailed his Ninety-Five Theses to the door of Wittenberg Castle Church on 31 October 1517. His dramatic criticisms of the excesses and corruptions of the Catholic Church would send shock waves throughout Christian Europe.

The Dutch theologian Erasmus shared Martin Luther's criticisms of the Church but differed in that he sought reform within the Church and claimed he was not attacking the very institution itself. For Luther, it was inevitable that breaks and schisms would occur within the Church and that they were likely to be accompanied by social disruption and change.

Protestant theologians attacked what they saw as the idolatrous worship of saints within Catholicism and called for an end to the superstition and hysteria that they believed had come to dominate their cults. Protestants argued that Christians should not make the mistake of treating saints as false idols to worship but should see them simply as admirable examples to follow. The most defining feature of this period is the conflict created between the Catholic Church and those who wanted to reform Christian practices. In this volatile and frequently violent period, faith and allegiances would be severely tested and the result was often the creation of new martyrs and saints.

St Thomas More

Today Thomas More ranks amongst a relatively small number of English saints who are widely acknowledged throughout the Roman Catholic Church and is amongst the most famous martyrs of the Reformation. He was born in London in 1478 and was the son of a barrister called Sir John More. As a boy of thirteen he was sent to the household of John Morton, the Archbishop of Canterbury. Morton placed him at Canterbury College in Oxford but his father recalled him to London. He was instead directed to a career in law and was called to the bar in 1501. He expressed interest in a religious vocation early on and considered joining the priesthood or the Friars Minor but, in the event, More did embark on a career as a lawyer.

He married his first wife Jane Colt in 1505 and had four children (three daughters called Margaret, Elizabeth and Cicely and a son named John) with her before her death in 1511. The couple also adopted a girl who had been orphaned called Margaret. Shortly after the death of his first wife More remarried a widow called Alice Middleton, primarily so that his children should not grow up without a mother in their lives. It has often been noted that More did not share the commonly held view of women of the society that he lived in and expended great time and effort upon the education of his daughters. He believed that men and women were of equal intelligence.

More's abilities were noticed by Henry VIII and he gave him the post of Under Sheriff of London in 1510. He later made him his envoy to Flanders in 1516 and, in the following year, More became a counsellor to the king. Following a diplomatic mission to the Holy Roman Emperor King Charles V on behalf of Henry VIII, More was awarded a knighthood. He was given the role of Speaker of the House of Commons in 1523. He also became known as the author of literary works, including the widely celebrated *Utopia*, written in 1515.

When the marriage of Henry VIII and Catherine of Aragon did not produce the son and heir that Henry wanted so desperately, the king took steps to seek an annulment. Henry's favour turned towards Anne Boleyn, a lady of the royal court. Cardinal Wolsey attempted to secure an annulment of their marriage from Pope Clement VII but, when his efforts proved unsuccessful, he provoked the displeasure of the king. Under pressure from Henry, Wolsey then left his post as Lord Chancellor. In 1529, Henry gave the position to Thomas More who was initially supportive of the king's claims that his marriage to Catherine had been unlawful. As Lord Chancellor he demonstrated a particular disgust for heretics, viewing them as a potentially destabilising danger to society. During Cardinal Wolsey's tenure as Lord Chancellor, More was active in helping stop books that contained Lutheran beliefs entering England. Whilst More is often viewed as pious, principled and particularly kind to his family, it should be remembered that he was also responsible for sentencing six Lutheran heretics to be burned to death whilst he was Lord Chancellor. He also showed no hesitation in having around forty more Lutheran sympathisers sent to prison.

However, although More was in many ways entirely committed to the authority of the monarch and believed in the importance of hierarchy and structure within society, it became increasingly obvious that Henry would not accept the authority of the pope.

When the king revealed that he planned to take on the role and powers traditionally held by the pope, More was horrified. It is, of course, the belief in the Roman Catholic Church that the popes are the direct successors to St Peter and therefore their importance as leaders of the Church is indisputable. King Henry VIII demanded that the clergy acknowledge him as the newly styled 'Protector and Supreme Head of the Church of England'. Although More was opposed to this and considered stepping down as Lord Chancellor, he was persuaded to stay by John Fisher and other religious figures who found themselves in a similar predicament. They took the oath demanded by the king that he should be acknowledged as head of the English Church with the additional proviso, 'as far as the law of Christ allows'. With the agreement of the king, More finally resigned from his post in 1532 on the grounds of ill health. But his convictions and loyalty to the king were to be finally tested and found wanting when he refused to attend the coronation of Anne Boleyn as the queen of England.

He was then attacked with false charges that he had taken bribes whilst in office but was found innocent of them.

However, on 13 April 1534, More was asked to take an oath in front of a commission organised by the king, stating that he accepted the Act of Succession. Through this parliamentary act, the marriage of Henry VIII and Catherine of Aragon was declared to be null and void and the king's marriage to Anne Boleyn valid. The act further stated that any children from their union would inherit the throne. It also demanded that the subjects of the king recognise that Parliament had the ultimate power in religious matters and not the pope. More could not agree to the repudiation of the pope and found the matter particularly difficult because Clement VII, the reigning pope, had recently given his verdict that the marriage of Henry VIII and Catherine of Aragon was, and always had been, a valid one.

Following his refusal to recognise the Act of Succession and its repercussions for the Church in England, More was imprisoned within the Tower of London under accusations of high treason. He was tried on 1 July 1535 in Westminster Hall. During the trial he defended his position by stating that no temporal man could be pre-eminent above the successors of St Peter, the popes of the Roman Catholic Church. He was found guilty of high treason by the judges who included relatives of Anne Boleyn. His original sentence was that he be hanged, drawn and quartered as a traitor. However, Henry VIII altered the sentence to beheading. More was executed on 6 July 1535 and is reported as having said that he died for the Church and was 'the king's good servant, but God's first'. After the execution, his head was displayed on London Bridge as a warning to other traitors. His daughter Margaret took it away after a month on public display. His body was buried in the chapel of St Peter ad Vincula at the Tower of London. He was widely seen outside England as a martyr to his faith and he was eventually beatified in 1886. This was followed in 1935 by his canonisation and he is venerated today in both the Roman Catholic Church and the Anglican Communion. He is regarded as a patron saint of occupations including civil servants, lawyers and politicians and of a number of places such as Virginia and Florida.

St John Fisher

Born in 1469, John Fisher was a mercer's son from Beverly in Humberside. He received a good education at Cambridge University where he excelled and was made a fellow of Michaelhouse, later to become Trinity College. He was to pursue a religious vocation and, in 1491, he was ordained as a priest. After a series of prestigious posts within the college he became the chaplain of Lady Margaret Beaufort. Working with Lady Margaret, he reformed Cambridge University and he became a professor of divinity. In 1504, Fisher became the chancellor of Cambridge University. In the same year he also became the bishop of Rochester, then the smallest see in England. Although more prestigious posts were offered to him, he chose Rochester partly because it allowed him to combine his academic pursuits with his religious responsibilities. He enjoyed a considerable reputation as a religious figure and was outspoken in criticising Protestantism, even writing four books condemning the beliefs of Martin Luther.

He was praised by Henry VIII for his work as bishop but provoked his anger when, in 1529, he argued that the marriage of Henry and Catherine of Aragon was valid and that no divorce could legally be granted to the king. In 1531, he also argued that Henry could not be the Supreme Head of the Church in England. Three years later, when he refused to take the Oath of Succession, he was arrested and held in the Tower of London. When Henry VIII declared that Fisher was no longer bishop of Rochester, Pope Paul III almost simultaneously nominated him as a cardinal. In a typical display of black humour, Henry is said to have remarked that, even if the pope was to send Fisher a red hat, he would not have a head to put it on. Fisher was found guilty of treason at his trial on 17 June 1535 and was beheaded shortly afterwards. He is said to have met his death bravely, declaring that he was dying for his faith and forgiving his executioner for his actions. He was canonised in 1935 and shares his feast day of 22 June with his fellow martyr St Thomas More.

St John Houghton

Amongst the 'Forty Martyrs of England and Wales' who were canonised by Pope Paul VI in 1970 for their defence of the Roman Catholic faith against the demands of Henry VIII, John Houghton ranks as one of the most prominent. He was born in 1487 into an important Essex family and, after studying law at Oxford University, became a priest. He served as priest for four years and then, in 1515, he became a monk, joining the Carthusian Order at Smithfield in London. After promotion through a number of roles within the order he was offered the post of prior of the Carthusian priory of Beauvale in Nottinghamshire. However, his time in this post was brief and he was brought back to London to serve as prior of the London Charterhouse.

As previously noted, Henry VIII introduced the Oath of Succession in 1534, demanding that all those who were loyal to him should take it. The motivation of this new legislature was, of course, to prove that his marriage to Catherine of

Aragon was void and therefore to be disregarded. Thus the daughter born to him by Anne Boleyn was the rightful successor to the throne. When the Carthusian Order was asked to take the oath, Houghton came into conflict with the tyrannical king. He attempted to avoid taking it and then went on to state that the marriage of Henry and Catherine could not be disregarded. The king moved quickly and Houghton and other Carthusians were imprisoned in the Tower of London. Attempts were made by the archbishop of York to persuade them that acceptance of the oath was not in contravention of their beliefs. They agreed in principle but added the ambiguous statement that they accepted to the extent that the law permitted it.

However, when it was demanded in 1535 that the Carthusians take an oath recognising Henry VIII as the Supreme Head on earth of the Church in England, they were faced, like many other religious figures, with a crisis of conscience and belief. Houghton held a meeting with the Vicar-General, Thomas Cromwell, accompanied by fellow Carthusian monks Prior Robert Lawrence and Augustine Webster with the aim of agreeing to a compromise position as they had done with the Oath of Succession. Cromwell was unsympathetic to their requests and demanded an unequivocal answer that they felt they could not give. In response to their reluctance to take the oath, they were imprisoned in the Tower of London. Houghton stood trial with other monks from his order at Westminster Hall and, under severe pressure from Cromwell, the jury found them to be guilty of treason. They were sentenced to be hung, drawn and quartered. They were taken to Tyburn to be executed on 4 May 1535. Houghton and his fellow Carthusians were offered a last-minute opportunity to take the oath and avoid their terrible sentence but they refused to do so. Over the course of the next couple of years, many of the remaining members of the Carthusian community took the oath in the face of the threat of death but some remained defiant. Horrifically, ten Carthusian monks who refused to take the oath were placed in Newgate Prison where they were left to die of starvation.

St Philip Howard

Just as the reign of Henry VIII had created martyrs in England for the Roman Catholic Church, so too did the reign of his daughter Elizabeth I. Prominent amongst these was Philip Howard, the earl of Arundel. Born in 1557, he was the eldest son of the Duke of Norfolk and was one of the highest-ranking aristocrats in England. He was the heir not only to the earldom of Arundel but also to five other baronies. He was raised as a protestant but the loyalty of his father to Queen Elizabeth was questioned when he offered to marry Mary Queen of Scots. The Duke of Norfolk was tried on a charge of high treason, pronounced guilty and subsequently executed in 1572. Although the treason of his father blackened the family name, Howard was given into the charge of Lord Burghley and he received a good education at Cambridge University.

Despite his family history, he went on to achieve favour at the court of Elizabeth I. However, in 1581, Howard took the decision to leave England and to become a Catholic. He had apparently been persuaded to embrace Catholicism by the arguments of the Jesuit priest and martyr Edmund Campion. He took a ship to Europe with his wife Anne Dacres, planning to start a new life and to convert to Catholicism. When his plan was discovered, the ship he was travelling on was stopped and he was placed under arrest. He was then held in the Tower of London by order of Elizabeth. Although he was cleared of treason, he was to face more accusations of disloyalty to the Queen in 1589. This time it was claimed that, when England had been faced with the naval threat of the Armada, Howard had actively prayed for a Spanish victory. Interestingly, the judges concluded that praying was not evidence of treason and yet still proclaimed his guilt and passed the death sentence. His life was spared although he was kept a prisoner by Elizabeth for the rest of his life. He died in 1595, primarily because of the privations of his imprisonment. He remained loyal to the Roman Catholic faith and was amongst the Forty Martyrs of England and Wales who were canonised by Pope Paul VI in 1970.

King Charles I

It may come as a surprise to many to learn that Charles I, the English monarch who was executed following the English Civil War, was canonised by the Church of England after the restoration of the monarchy. He was born on 19 November 1600 and was the second son of James VI, King of Scotland and Anne of Denmark and Norway. He caused considerable controversy when, on 11 May 1625, he married Henrietta Maria of France who was a Roman Catholic. His coronation took place on 2 February 1626 amidst concerns that privately he had Roman Catholic sympathies.

Like his father, who became James I of England, Charles believed in the Divine Right of Kings, arguing that, as a king, he was ultimately answerable only to God. He also caused consternation to many by linking himself to a number of controversial ecclesiastical figures. When the cleric Richard Montagu was attacked in parliament by Puritans for a pamphlet he had written that criticised John Calvin he appealed to the king for assistance. In response, Charles I made Montagu a royal chaplain, a move that convinced many Puritans that his real sympathies lay with the Catholic Church.

The king also went on to appoint William Laud as Archbishop of Canterbury in 1633 and the new archbishop made a number of reforms aimed at directing the Church of England back to a more traditional form of worship that many viewed as being too close to Roman Catholicism. Laud's dislike of Calvinism caused much hostility towards the archbishop and the king and, when Charles I attempted to foist religious changes on Scotland, it resulted in the Bishops' Wars. Most dramatically, he became involved in a conflict with parliament that led to the English Civil War between 1642 and 1645. His enemies included the parliamentarians who fought against the king's attempts to increase his control over the country and Puritans alienated by his reforms and beliefs. After losing the war, Charles I refused to give in and to accept a constitutional monarchy and provoked a second war that lasted from 1648 to 1649 that also failed. He was then charged with trying to rule without Parliament (effectively as a tyrant) and with making war upon his own subjects.

Charles was brought to trial, charged with high treason, and faced a High Court of Justice specially created to try him by act of parliament. The trial began on 20 January 1649 but Charles, believing that his power and rights as king had been given to him by God, refused to enter a plea and argued that no court could hold power over a reigning monarch. Nonetheless the court found him guilty of the charges made against him and his death warrant was signed on 29 January 1649. The execution was carried out on the following day and he was beheaded in front of the Banqueting House of the

Palace of Westminster. In an account of the execution written twelve years after it had taken place, the royalist Philip Henry claimed that, after the king had been decapitated, the assembled crowd had let out a collective moan. He also claimed that some of the crowd had put the king's blood onto their handkerchiefs in an act of reverence. Usually, when traitors were executed, their heads were held up to the crowd and they were loudly and publicly declared to be a traitor. On this occasion nothing was said and, unusually, Oliver Cromwell allowed the severed head of the king to be sewed back on to the body. This allowed his family to pay their respects to Charles I and to give him a private burial at the Chapel of St George at Windsor Castle.

Following the restoration of the Monarchy and Church in 1660, the name of King Charles I was added to the calendar in the Book of Common Prayer by his son Charles II. In this context, he was referred to as St Charles, King and Martyr, and the Anglican Church celebrated the date of his execution as his feast day. However, during the reign of Queen Victoria, this was removed from the calendar and today it has the status of a lesser festival.

Saints in the Modern Era

Saints have clearly continued to act as intercessors between people and God in the modern era but their influence has extended far beyond the sphere of religion and belief into the secular world. The legends and stories attached to saints and their feast days have become a rich source of inspiration for business and commerce to such an extent that, in some cases, their original identities have been almost entirely obscured.

The veneration of Catholic saints has travelled into other cultures with sometimes unexpected results. As in the past, the selection of individuals to be recommended for sainthood has often been influenced by political concerns and has, at times, reflected the impact of important and traumatic events upon society. The process of canonisation has also undergone some reform but, perhaps surprisingly, it remains fundamentally unchanged. The choice of candidates for sainthood, from the Romanov family murdered during the Russian revolution to Mother Teresa, has occasionally polarised opinion and caused considerable controversy.

Santeria/Voodoo

The enforced transportation of slaves from Africa to the New World has had a huge impact on world history and culture and its consequences have been enormous. However, one of the strangest and perhaps most unexpected was the creation of what could be termed a whole new religion. West Africans taken from their homelands to work in the sugar plantations of the Caribbean were also made to convert to Catholicism and forced to abandon their own traditional beliefs and religious practices. Clearly, such oppression often has the effect of forcing ideas and practices underground and, rather than give up their own rituals and religions, slave communities simply disguised them.

Traditional West African religions involved the worship of nature and deities termed as 'orishas'. The slaves brought to work on plantations appeared to embrace the Roman Catholic religion of their owners but, in fact, continued their own religious practices. They simply substituted public reverence for the pantheon of Catholic saints for the worship of their own gods. When slaves seemed to be celebrating the feast days of the saints it was, in fact, a front for the worship of orishas. This bias in favour of devotion to the saints was recognised by slave owners who termed their worship as 'Santeria'. It is an insulting term intended to describe forms of Catholicism that overemphasise the importance of the saints. Within Christianity in general, the saints are not, of course, viewed as greater than God and they are not to be worshipped as Gods or false idols. Arguably, the development of Santeria was far from the first time that Christianity had been merged with elements of pre-Christian religions. An interesting earlier example is the popularity of the pre-Christian fertility figure of the Green Man whose image appears in many Western medieval churches.

Church of Latter Day Saints

It is the belief of the Church of Latter Day Saints, more commonly known as Mormons, that, following the death of St Peter and the other apostles, the Church moved away from the original teachings of Jesus Christ. The term 'Latter Day' indicates that Mormons believe that they are living in a time when the second coming of Jesus Christ is imminent. The Church of Latter Day Saints also believes that the biblical prophecy of Malachi that Elijah would return to earth before the coming of the messiah has, in fact, already taken place. According to the Latter Day Saints, Elijah met Joseph Smith Jr, the founder of their movement, on 3 April 1836. They met at the Kirtland Temple and the prophet announced that the coming of the Lord was imminent.

Romanov Saints

In 1981, members of the Romanov family of Tsar Nicholas II, murdered during the Russian Revolution, were canonised as holy martyrs by the Russian Orthodox Church Abroad. Along with Tsar Nicholas II, Tsarina Alexandra, their children Tatiana, Olga, Anastasia and Alexei, other members of the Romanov family were also canonised. They were the sister of Tsarina Alexandra, the Grand Duchess Elizabeth Fyodorovna and Sister Varvar Yakovleva who was her companion, Prince Igor Konstantinovich, Prince Ioann Konstantinovich of Russia, Prince Konstantin Konstantinovich of Russia, Prince Vladimir Pavlovich Paley and Grand Duke Sergey Mikhaylovich of Russia and Fyodor Remez, his secretary.

A number of their servants were also canonised. These included a footman called Alexei Trupp, court physician Yevgeny

Botkin, Alexandra's maid Anna Demidova and the family cook Ivan Kharitonov. These servants had been killed with the Romanov family by the Bolsheviks on 17 July 1918. A further two individuals who had served the tsar and tsarina and who were murdered later in 1918 were a tutor called Catherine Adolphovna Schneider and Anastasia Hendrikova, a lady-in-waiting. They were described as victims oppressed by the Soviet State by the Russian Orthodox Church Abroad.

Following the dramatic social and political changes within the Soviet Union, the cultural climate had changed to the extent that, in the year 2000, the Romanovs were officially recognised and canonised by the Russian Orthodox Church as passion bearers. A passion bearer within the Russian Orthodox Church is a Christian individual who has died righteously at the hands of others. Although the Romanov family were declared to be passion bearers, their servants were not accorded that status. On 17 July 1998, the remains of the tsar and tsarina were laid to rest in St Petersburg at the St Peter and Paul Cathedral. The bodies of three of the Romanov daughters were also buried with their parents on the same day. Another dramatic example of world events leading to the creation of new saints is the persecution of priests and Roman Catholic worshippers during the Spanish Civil War between 1934 and 1939. It has been estimated that as many as 6,832 Catholics were murdered during the course of the war. A number of these victims were canonised by Pope John Paul II in 1999 and the feast day of the Martyrs of the Spanish Civil War is held on 9 October.

Congregation for the Causes of Saints

As we have seen, in the early Christian Church the process whereby individuals were accorded the status of sainthood was largely one of popular and local acclaim. This informal system became increasingly centralised by the Catholic Church over time until the granting of sainthood came under the power of the papacy itself. It is now thought that this papal prerogative to canonise certain individuals was formalised by Pope Innocent III (1199–1216), building on the groundwork already carried out by previous popes. Today, the body within the Roman Catholic Church that oversees the canonisation of saints is known as *Congregatio de Causis Sanctorum* or the Sacred Congregation for the Causes of Saints.

Previously, Pope Sixtus V had formed the Sacred Congregation for Rites in 1588, a body that both dealt with the canonisation of saints and acted as a regulator for practises of worship within the Church. Pope Benedict XIV wrote an important work on the subject of canonisation called *De servorum Dei beatificatione et beatorum canonizatione* between 1734 and 1738 which set the generally accepted precedent for the process. It came to be accepted that there were three main stages or grades in the process of canonisation. In the first, the individual was termed the 'Venerable servant of God', in the second 'blessed' and finally he or she was designated a 'saint'. Local churches are expected to call for the recognition of important individuals in this way and in order for someone to be beatified and declared 'blessed' they must demonstrate evidence of what is termed 'heroic virtue'. When the candidate has been beatified they can then be venerated at a local level. In some cases, achieving sainthood may take centuries and has, at times, required evidence of miracles performed by the candidate. However, martyrs fall outside this category and evidence of miracles may not be necessary. When the individual has been accorded the status of saint then he or she can be formally venerated on a universal level.

However, in 1969, Pope Paul VI took the decision to divide the Sacred Congregation for Rites into two separate bodies, the Congregation for the Divine Worship and the Congregation for the Causes of Saints. Pope John Paul II made further important changes to the process of awarding sainthood in 1983. His reforms were aimed at speeding up and simplifying the process of canonisation. Following the changes implemented by John Paul II, the process has two main stages. An investigation is carried out into the life of the proposed individual and any attendant miracles they are thought to have performed at diocesan level. Written evidence is gathered which may include evidence submitted by eyewitnesses given in a court presided over by the bishop. Secondly, following this process and the resulting preparation of a documented report, the case is put before the Roman congregation. This committee of expert theologians examines the case in detail and reaches a decision as to whether or not they recommend canonisation. If the conclusion is reached that the committee should recommend canonisation then they will put the case before the pope himself. The pope will then reach a decision upon the matter.

Mother Teresa

Perhaps the most famous case of a modern individual whom the Roman Catholic Church has taken steps to canonise is the Albanian nun and missionary Mother Teresa. Born in 1910 in Skopje, Mother Teresa is today best known for her humanitarian work amongst the poor and sick in Calcutta in India. Her birth name was Agnes Gonxha Bojaxhiu and, from a young age, she appeared to have a calling to a religious life. At the age of eighteen, she became a missionary with the Sisters of Loreto. Before departing for India to work as a missionary she spent some time in Ireland where she learned to speak and write in English. As a missionary she would teach Indian children lessons in English. In 1929 she travelled to India and, two years later, she undertook her first vows as a nun, changing her name to Teresa in emulation of St Teresa of Lisieux who is regarded as the patron saint of missionaries.

Mother Teresa made her solemn vows to the Sisters of Loreto in 1937 and she worked as a teacher for them in Calcutta. However, whilst she worked hard and diligently in this capacity, she apparently felt an increasing sense that she should pursue a different course as a missionary. Appalled and shocked by the poverty and suffering that she encountered within Calcutta, she decided to leave the convent and the relative security and comfort that it offered her and work and live amongst the poor. In 1948, she left the convent to work as a missionary in the poorest sections of the city. Although she experienced much hardship and difficulty at the beginning of this work, she was to receive the support of the papacy. Without funding or supplies her earliest work had been supported through begging but, in 1950, the Vatican authorised the setting up of a diocesan congregation in Calcutta. It was founded as a small order of only thirteen members and the purpose of its work was to care for the outcast members of society whom all other agencies had effectively abandoned. Mother Teresa opened the famous Home for the Dying in 1952 in a former Hindu temple. The order that Mother Teresa founded would become known as the Missionaries of Charity.

The Missionaries of Charity also opened homes to care for people suffering from leprosy and, as their work came to international attention, the order attracted volunteers and financial assistance.

As the fame of Mother Teresa's work became more widespread, the Missionaries of Charity began to undertake work in other areas of India and, eventually, in dozens of other countries around the world. Mother Teresa personally carried out missionary work in Beirut and former Soviet countries as well as in Ethiopia and in her home country of Albania. In later life, Mother Teresa was troubled by heart problems that impacted on her health. In 1983 she had a heart attack in Rome and another followed six years later. However, she continued to work as the head of the Missionaries of Charity until 1997 when finally her poor health made continuing impossible. She died later that same year on 5 September.

Since the death of Mother Teresa, the Holy See has begun the process that may ultimately lead to her canonisation. One of the major events in this process was the recognition by the Vatican in 2002 of a miracle relating to Mother Teresa. A woman called Monica Besra claimed that, when she was suffering from an abdominal tumour, it had been healed by a beam of light that had shone from a locket holding a picture of Mother Teresa. Because of this miracle, Mother Teresa has been beatified by the Roman Catholic Church but she has not yet been canonised. However, other witnesses argued that hospital treatment saved the woman and not divine intervention. Acclaim for Mother Teresa has not been universal. She has also been criticised by a number of people, including the author Christopher Hitchens, who argued that her motivating principle was not to relieve misery and suffering but to recruit new converts to the Catholic Faith.

St Nicholas

Perhaps no single saint has undergone a greater change in identity in the modern world than St Nicholas. This important Christian figure, who is particularly venerated in the Eastern Church, has been radically transformed in the Western world into the ubiquitous yet slightly bizarre character of Santa Claus. Very little is known about the life of St Nicholas other than that he lived during the fourth century AD and was Bishop of Myra. His bishopric was located in what is now modern day Turkey in the province of Antalya. During his lifetime the Eastern Roman, or Byzantine, Empire ruled the region. His cult is an ancient one with evidence of his veneration dating from the sixth century AD. His name in Greek means 'victory of the people'. In 1087, his relics were removed from Anatolia because of Muslim invasions and taken to southern Italy where a new shrine was built for them at Bari. Pope Urban II oversaw the official ceremony of the inauguration of the relics of St Nicholas at the new church. The translation of the saint's relics to Bari greatly boosted his popularity in Western Europe where he became widely known and revered.

The miracles attributed to the saint in later stories of his life led to him becoming a patron saint of children, sailors, pawnbrokers, merchants and many other occupations. St Nicholas is said to have been born into a wealthy family and to have demonstrated an early interest in religion as a child. In religious art, St Nicholas is sometimes shown as an infant refusing to drink milk from his mother's breasts on Wednesdays and Fridays as an act of fledgling piety because these were days of canonical fasting.

According to legend, St Nicholas saved three girls from

prostitution by giving each of them three bags of gold to serve as their marriage dowries. Their father was unable to pay for their weddings and the intervention of St Nicholas saved them from a life of poverty and sin. It has been claimed that this story of the saint helping the poor is the origin of pawnbrokers adopting the symbol of the three golden balls hung outside pawnshops.

In another story, he saves three sailors from drowning and three innocent men from execution. Another legend has him resurrect three boys who had been murdered by a butcher in a tub of brine. Interestingly, a later version of this legend tells that the butcher let three clerks stay the night at his house and killed them all. He then hid his crime by turning their remains into meat pies to sell in his shop. It may be that this medieval version of the story was the inspiration for the later story of Sweeney Todd, the Demon Barber of Fleet Street. In any event, St Nicholas is reputed to have discovered the crime of the murdered clerks and resurrected them.

He is also said to have destroyed a number of pagan temples and to have been a vociferous opponent of the Arian heresy. Interestingly, the feast day of St Nicholas is 6 December which was also the date celebrated in the ancient world as the birth of the goddess Diana or Artemis. St Nicholas is reported to have destroyed a temple dedicated to Diana and it has been argued that the choice of his feast day was an attempt to eclipse its previous pre-Christian significance. Some sources claim that Justinian I, emperor of the Eastern Roman Empire, caused a church to be built and dedicated in honour of St Nicholas in the city of Constantinople, then the capital of the Eastern Empire. When the saint's relics were held at Myra, it was claimed that they exuded a sticky, sweet substance called manna or myrrh that had powerful properties. When the relics were translated to Bari by Italian sailors, they apparently continued to do so. It is for this reason that St Nicholas is also the patron saint of perfumiers.

In the low countries of Europe it became traditional for sailors to give gifts on 6 December, the feast day of St Nicholas, their patron saint. Because of the story of his resurrection of the three murdered boys and because of his reputation for giving gifts derived from the story of the three girls and their dowries, St Nicholas was also regarded as the patron saint of children. Thus, it also became traditional to give gifts to children on his feast day. These elements of the cult of St Nicholas later became intertwined with earlier pre-Christian traditions and particularly stories and legends relating to the Norse god Odin. These folk traditions were carried to America by Dutch Protestants who settled in New Amsterdam and who referred to St Nicholas as 'Sinterklaas'. Over time, the legends associated with St Nicholas arrived in Britain where he became known as Father Christmas.

St Valentine

Today St Valentine's Day, for most people, is synonymous with the concepts of love, romance and courtship. It is a day on which lovers send one another valentine's cards and exchange gifts and, in modern times, it has become an increasingly commercialised event. Historically, it became an opportunity for the mass production of valentine's cards, particularly in America during the mid-nineteenth century. Like many other aspects of the cults of the saints, it has become an integral, perhaps unquestioned aspect of daily life and has become an accepted part of western culture and traditions. However, the origin of St Valentine's Day is a particularly obscure and tangled one and has caused a degree of disagreement and controversy amongst religious scholars and historians.

The early martyrologies list three saints named Valentine who died as martyrs for their faith as sharing their feast day on 14 February. Little is known of their lives, which adds to the confusion surrounding the origin of St Valentine's Day, but the three men are said to be a Valentine of Rome, a Valentine of Terni and another Valentine who was martyred in Africa. St Valentine of Rome was a priest who was martyred in around 269 AD and was buried alongside the route of the Flaminian Way. His relics were later transferred and claimed by the Church of Saint Praxed in Rome. However, from 1835, the White Friar Carmelite Church in Dublin has also claimed to hold his relics.

St Valentine of Terni was a bishop of Interamna, today the modern city of Terni, and he also is said to have been martyred in the second half of the third century and to have been buried at a different spot along the course of the Flaminian Way. His relics were transferred to the Basilica of St Valentine in Terni at a later date and, it is claimed, they are held there still. The identity of the third St Valentine has survived only through early written accounts and nothing further is known of his life or final resting place. A group of religious scholars known as the Bollandists have claimed that Valentine of Rome and Valentine of Terni were, in fact, the same person.

It is perhaps worth adding that the name Valentine was a common one in the later Roman Empire and has its root in the name Valens, meaning 'worthy'. Famous examples of individuals from this period whose names share this origin include the brothers Valentinian and Valens who ruled as Western and Eastern Emperors respectively during the fourth century AD. However, no early accounts of the various candidates named as St Valentine contain reference to love and romance and what is recorded is similar to the lives of many other early Christian martyrs. They were simply pious individuals who were killed by intolerant Roman emperors because of their religious beliefs.

It has been widely argued that the tradition of St Valentine's Day was an attempt by the Christian Church to supersede the ancient pagan festival of Lupercalia that took place in the city of Rome on 15 February. Lupercalia was a fertility festival that appears to have had its roots in the myth of Romulus and Remus, the founders of the city of Rome. According to legend, Romulus and Remus were suckled by a she-wolf in a cave near to Rome. The name of the festival of Lupercalia is linked to the Latin word for wolf, 'lupus', and this legend was the focus of a local cult and the site of the cave was known as the 'lupercal'. Cult members would traditionally sacrifice a dog and two goats and the blood would be sprinkled in the streets. The purpose of this was apparently to promote fertility and to ward off roaming wolves. It was also the practice of youths to run naked in the city of Rome in a festive and jovial atmosphere, hitting those they met with thongs in the belief that this would aid the conception of children and giving birth to them. Similarly, in ancient Greece, the religious phase around the time of St Valentine's Day was linked to the subject of sex, love and fertility. This period was known as 'Gamelion' and recognised the marriage of the god Zeus and the goddess Hera.

Interestingly, Pope Gelasius I was responsible both for banning the festival of Lupercalia and also for officially declaring, in 496 AD, that 14 February was the feast day of St Valentine. However, he simultaneously acknowledged that almost nothing was known about the saints but he included their names in his list of those saints that he believed to have died as martyrs for the Christian faith. The author Henry Ansgar Kelly has argued that the first clear linking of the celebration of St Valentine's Day with the subject of love was made during the Middle Ages by Geoffrey Chaucer, author of *The Canterbury Tales*. In a poem of around 1381 entitled 'The Parliament of Fowls', Chaucer claims that it was believed at this time that, during the middle of February, birds would make pairs and choose a mate. Chaucer wrote the poem to celebrate the engagement of King Richard II of England to Anne of Bohemia. The poem contains the lines:

> For this was sent on Seynt Valentine's day
> Whan every foul cometh ther to choose his mate.

Kelly has argued that Chaucer was simply using a literary convention of the day in associating the subject with the feast day of a saint. It may also be that he was actually referring to the feast day of St Valentine of Genoa that takes place on 2 May.

Confusing though all this may be, it does appear to have been the recognisable beginning of the widely held belief that St Valentine's Day is a day for lovers.

Commercial Saints

The commercial exploitation of the veneration of saints that can be seen in the transformation of the roles of St Nicholas and St Valentine can be recognised elsewhere in modern society. An interesting recent example of the Catholic Church condemning it has involved an Italian company sending virtual prayer cards to mobile phone owners. Those who subscribe to the service will receive as many as three images of saints and other important Catholic figures including various popes and the Virgin Mary. The cost of the virtual prayer card service is three euros a week. However, a conference of Italian bishops on 4 December 2007 concluded that the service was blasphemous and exploitative. Bishop Lucio Soravito De Franceshi speaking on behalf of the conference members commented that, 'this is a poor show and has nothing to do with faith. It is exploiting the faith, lowering it to banality with no sense. It is a blasphemous idea that will horrify the true faithful. For the church a saint is someone of great heroic virtue, not someone to be commercially exploited.' (*The Daily Telegraph*, Wednesday, 5 December 2007, p.20)

In response to the criticisms the director of the company, Barbara Labate said, 'I don't think it's scandalous or blasphemous at all. We have had saint and prayer cards for more than 600 years and we will continue to have them. What we are doing is moving with the times.' (*The Daily Telegraph*, Wednesday, 5 December 2007, p.20) Whilst it is difficult to believe that the main motivation for the provision of the virtual prayer cards is anything other than commercial, it is tempting to say that they are simply continuing a long standing tradition in which the veneration of saints becomes a source for the creation of revenue. During the Middle Ages many monasteries and churches valued the relics of saints that they held because it meant a constant stream of pilgrims to their shrines. There are numerous instances of churches searching out the relics of saints in order to become important pilgrimage sites. One such example is the translation of the relics of St Winifride in 1138 from North Wales to Shrewsbury Abbey in Shropshire. The abbey was founded in the wake of the Norman Conquest and actively searched for the relics of a saint in order to increase its spiritual importance and significance as a focus for pilgrimage. It became a popular destination for Christians who would travel first to Shrewsbury to pray at the shrine of St Winifride and then continue on to Holywell in Clywd, North Wales, another site linked to the Welsh saint. It became such an important shrine that, in 1416, Henry V travelled on foot from Shrewsbury to Holywell. King Edward IV is another English monarch who is also said to have taken this important journey.

Today, as in the past, saints continue to fascinate, inspire and appal us. Their lives and actions have become part of the fabric of society from place names to significant dates in the ritual and secular year. Whilst they continue to serve as an important focus for religious belief, their influence has also permeated into all levels of popular culture. One answer as to why this is so may be because they tap into enduring concerns and mythic cycles that resonate as much with people today as they did in the ancient and medieval worlds.

Appendices

A Calendar of Saints' Days

Below is a calendar of saints that is not intended to be either exhaustive or all-encompassing but instead to represent the major feast days as well as offering a diverse and varied range of saints from different cultures and traditions.

January 1	Blessed Virgin Mary
	St Joseph Tomasi
	St Odilo
January 2	St Basil the Great
	St Gregory of Nazianzus
January 3	St Genevieve
January 4	St Pharaildis
January 5	St Simeon Stylites
January 6	St Peter of Canterbury
January 7	St Raymond of Penafort
January 8	St Thorfinn
January 9	St Adrian
January 10	St Peter Orseolo
January 11	St Vitalis of Gaza
January 12	St Benedict
January 13	St Hilary of Poitiers
January 14	St Sava

January 15	St Ita
January 16	St Honoratus
January 17	St Anthony Abbot
January 18	St Ulfrid
January 19	St Wulfstan
January 20	St Sebastian
January 21	St Agnes
January 22	St Vincent of Saragossa
January 23	St John the Almsgiver
January 24	St Francis de Sales
January 25	St Dwyn
January 26	St Paula
January 27	St Angela Merici
January 28	St Thomas Aquinas
January 29	St Gildas
January 30	St Martina
January 31	St Aidan
February 1	St Brigid of Ireland
February 2	St Joan de Lestonnac
February 3	St Blaise
February 4	St John de Britto
February 5	St Agatha
February 6	St Amand
February 7	St Luke the Younger
February 8	St Jerome Emiliani
February 9	St Teilo
February 10	St Scholastica
February 11	St Caedmon
February 12	St Julian the Hospitaller
February 13	St Modomnoc
February 14	St Valentine

February 15	St Sigfrid
February 16	St Juliana
February 17	St Fintan
February 18	St Fra Angelico
February 19	St Boniface
February 20	St Wulfric
February 21	St Peter Damian
February 22	St Margaret of Cortona
February 23	St Polycarp
February 24	St Prix
February 25	St Ethelbert of Kent
February 26	St Alexander
February 27	St Gabriel Possenti
February 28	St Romanus
March 1	St David
March 2	St Chad
March 3	St Cunegund
March 4	St Casimir of Poland
March 5	St Piran
March 6	St Colette
March 7	St Drausius
March 8	St John of God
March 9	St Frances of Rome
March 10	St Kessog
March 11	St Oengus
March 12	St Theophanes the Chronicler
March 13	St Ansovinus
March 14	St Leobinus
March 15	St Louise de Marillac
March 16	St Herbert
March 17	St Patrick

March 18	St Cyril
March 19	St Joseph
March 20	St Cuthbert
March 21	St Enda
March 22	St Nicholas Owen
March 23	St Turibius
March 24	St Irenaeus
March 25	St Dismas
March 26	St Ludger
March 27	St John of Egypt
March 28	St Gontran
March 29	St Rupert
March 30	St Zosimus
March 31	St Balbina
April 1	St Catherine of Palma
April 2	St Francis of Paolo
April 3	St Irene
April 4	St Isidore
April 5	St Vincent Ferrer
April 6	St William of Eskilsoe
April 7	St John Baptist de la Salle
April 8	St Walter of Pontnoise
April 9	St Hedda of Peterborough
April 10	St Fulbert
April 11	St Stanislaus of Poland
April 12	St Zeno
April 13	St Hermenegild
April 14	St Benezet
April 15	St Hunna
April 16	St Magnus of Orkney
April 17	St Stephen Harding

April 18	St Aya
April 19	St Alphege
April 20	St Caedwalla
April 21	St Anselm
April 22	St Theodore of Sykeon
April 23	St George
April 24	St Fidelis
April 26	St Marcellinus
April 27	St Zita
April 28	St Peter Mary Chanel
April 29	St Catherine of Siena
April 30	St Wolfhard
May 1	St Asaph
May 2	St Athanasius
May 3	St James the Lesser
	St Philip
May 4	St Florian
May 5	St Hilary
May 6	St Petronax
May 7	St Domitian
May 8	St Peter of Tarentaise
May 9	St Pachomius
May 10	St Cathal
May 11	St Francis di Girolama
May 12	St Pancras
May 13	St Imelda
May 14	St Matthias
May 15	St Isidore the Farmer
May 16	St Brendan the Navigator
May 17	St Madron
May 18	St Theodotus

May 19	St Dunstan
May 20	St Bernadino of Siena
May 21	St Andrew Bobola
May 22	St Rita
May 23	St Didier
May 24	St Sara
	St Vincent of Lerin
	St David of Scotland
May 25	St Bede
May 26	St Philip Neri
May 27	St Augustine of Canterbury
May 28	St Germain (Germanus)
May 29	St Alexander
May 30	St Joan of Arc
May 31	St Petronilla
June 1	St Justin
June 2	St Elmo
June 3	St Charles Lwanga
June 4	St Petroc
June 5	St Boniface of Mainz
June 6	St Norbert
June 7	St Meriadoc
June 8	St William
June 9	St Columba
June 10	St Ithamar
June 11	St Barnabus
June 12	St John of Sahagun
June 13	St Antony of Padua
June 14	St Dogmael
June 15	St Vitus
June 16	St Cyricus

June 17	St Rainerius of Pisa
June 18	St Elizabeth of Schonau
June 19	St Romuald
June 20	St Alban
June 21	St Aloysius
June 22	St John Fisher
	St Thomas More
June 23	St Audrey
June 24	St John the Baptist
June 25	St Eurosia
June 26	St Anthelm
June 27	St Cyril
June 28	St Irenaeus
June 29	St Paul
	St Peter
June 30	St Martial of Limoges
July 1	St Oliver Plunket
July 2	St Oudoceus
July 3	St Thomas
July 4	St Ulric
July 5	St Morwenna
	St Athanasius of Athos
July 6	St Sexburga
July 7	St Palladius
July 8	St Kilian
July 9	St Veronica Giuliani
July 10	St Canute
July 11	St Benedict
July 12	St Veronica
July 13	St Henry the Emperor of Finland

July 14	St Camillus
July 15	St Swithin
July 16	St Helier
July 17	St Alexis
July 18	St Arnulf
July 19	St Macrina the Younger
July 20	St Margaret of Antioch
July 21	St Laurence of Brindisi
July 22	St Mary Magdalene
July 23	St Bridget of Sweden
July 24	St Christina the Astonishing
July 25	St Christopher
	St James the Great
July 26	St Anne
July 27	St Pantaleon
July 28	St Samson
July 29	St Olaf
	St Lupus
July 30	St Tatwin
July 31	St Ignatius of Loyola
August 1	St Alphonsus
August 2	St Etheldritha
August 3	St Lydia
August 4	St Sithney
August 5	St Cassyon
August 6	St Justus
	St Pastor
August 7	St Cajetan
August 8	St Dominic
August 9	St Oswald of Northumbria
August 10	St Lawrence

August 11	St Clare
August 12	St Murtagh
August 13	St Hippolytus
August 14	St Maximilian Kolbe
August 15	St Tarcisius
August 16	St Armel
August 17	St Hyacinth
August 18	St Helena
August 19	St Mochta
August 20	St Bernard of Clairvaux
August 21	St Pius X
August 22	St Philip Benizi
August 23	St Rose of Lima
August 24	St Bartholomew
August 25	St Genesius
August 26	St Ninian
August 27	St Monica
August 28	St Augustine of Hippo
August 29	St Edwold
August 30	St Fiacre
August 31	St Raymond Nonnatus
September 1	St Giles
September 2	St William of Roskilde
September 3	St Gregory the Great
September 4	St Rosalia
September 5	St Laurence Gustiani
September 6	St Bega
September 7	St Tilbert
September 8	St Adrian
September 9	St Peter Claver
September 10	St Nicholas of Tolentino

September 11	St Protus
	St Hyacinth
September 12	St Ailbe
September 13	St John Chrysostom
September 14	St Notburga
September 15	St Catherine of Genoa
September 16	St Cyprian
September 17	St Lambert
September 18	St Joseph of Copertino
September 19	St Januarius
September 20	St Eustace
September 21	St Matthew
September 22	St Maurice
September 23	St Adamnan
September 24	St Gerard
September 25	St Albert
September 26	St Cosmas
	St Damian
September 27	St Vincent de Paul
September 28	St Wenceslaus of Bohemia
September 29	St Michael and All Angels
September 30	St Jerome
October 1	St Remi
	St Teresa of Lisieux
October 2	The Guardian Angels
October 3	St Thomas Cantilupe
October 4	St Francis of Assisi
October 5	St Placid
October 6	St Bruno
October 7	St Osyth
October 8	St Demetrius

October 9	St Denis
October 10	St Victor
October 11	St Gomer
October 12	St Wilfrid of York
October 13	St Edward the Confessor
October 14	St Callistus
October 15	St Teresa of Avila
October 16	St Margaret Mary
October 17	St Ignatius of Antioch
October 18	St Luke
October 19	Jesuit Martyrs of Canada
October 20	St Paul of the Cross
October 21	St Hilarion
October 22	St Donatus
October 23	St John of Capistrano
October 24	St Raphael
	St Anthony Claret
October 25	St Crispin and St Crispinian
	St Front of Périgueux
October 26	St Cedd
October 27	St Frumentius
October 28	St Simon
	St Jude
October 29	St Baldus
October 30	St Dorothy of Montau
October 31	St Quentin
November 1	All Saints
	St Marcel of Paris
November 2	St Marcian
November 3	St Martin de Porres
November 4	St Charles Borromeo

November 5	St Bertilla
November 6	St Illtud
	St Leonard
November 7	St Willibrord
November 8	Four Crowned Martyrs
	St Godfrey
November 9	St Benen
	St Theodore
November 10	St Leo the Great
November 11	St Martin of Tours
November 12	St Émilion
	St Josaphat
November 13	St Francis Xavier Cabrini
November 14	St Lawrence O'Toole of Dublin
November 15	St Albert the Great
November 16	St Margaret of Scotland
November 17	St Elizabeth of Hungary
	St Gregory of Tours
November 18	St Odo of Cluny
November 19	St Nerses
November 20	St Edmund the Martyr
November 21	St Albert of Louvain
November 22	St Cecilia
November 23	St Columban
November 24	St Colman of Cloyne
November 25	St Catherine of Alexandria
	St Mercurius (Mercury)
November 26	St Silvester Gozzolini
November 27	St Virgil
November 28	St Catherine Labouré
November 29	St Sernin
November 30	St Andrew

December 1	St Edmund Campion
December 2	St Chromatius
December 3	St Francis Xavier
December 4	St Barbara
	St Osmund
December 5	St Sabas
December 6	St Nicholas
December 7	St Ambrose
December 8	St Romaric
December 9	St Leocadia
December 10	St Eulalia
December 11	St Damasus
December 12	St Vicelin
December 13	St Judoc
December 14	St John of the Cross
	St Spiridon
December 15	St Nino
December 16	St Adelaide
December 17	St Lazurus
December 18	St Flannan
December 19	St Anastasius I
December 20	St Dominic of Silos
December 21	St Peter Canisius
December 22	St Chaeremon
December 23	St John of Kanti
December 24	St Irmina
	St Adela
December 25	St Anastasia
December 26	St Stephen
December 27	St John the Divine
December 28	St Antony of Lérins
December 29	St Thomas Becket

December 30   St Egwin
December 31   St Silvester I

Patron Saints of Occupations

Accountants	St Matthew
Actors	St Genesius
Artists	St Fra Angelico
Archers	St George, St Sebastian
Astronomers	St Dominic
Athletes	St Dominic
Authors	St Francis of Sales
Bakers	St Nicholas
Bankers	St Matthew
Beggars	St Giles
Blacksmiths	St Dunstan
Bee keepers	St Bernard of Clairvaux
Booksellers	St John of God
Brewers	St Augustine of Hippo
Bricklayers	St Stephen
Builders	St Vincent Ferrer
Carpenters	St Joseph
Comedians	St Vitus
Cooks	St Martha
Dancers	St Vitus
Dentists	St Apollonia
Doctors	St Cosmas
	St Damian
Ecologists	St Francis of Assisi
Farmers	St George
Firefighters	St Florian
Fishermen	St Andrew
Florists	St Teresa of Lisieux
Funeral Directors	St Joseph of Arimathea
Goldsmiths	St Dunstan
Gravediggers	St Anthony Abbot

Grocers	St Michael
Hairdressers	St Martin de Porres
Hermits	St Giles
Hoteliers	St Amand
Housewives	St Martha
Husbandmen	St George
Journalists	St Francis of Sales
Knights	St George
Labourers	St Isidore
Librarians	St Catherine of Alexandria
Locksmiths	St Quentin
Messengers	St Gabriel the Archangel
Miners	St Anne
Musicians	St Cecilia
Nurses	Blessed Virgin Mary
Painters	St Luke
Paratroopers	St Michael
Pawnbrokers	St Nicholas
Poets	St Columba
Police	St Michael
Politicians	St Thomas More
Postal workers	St Gabriel the Archangel
Publishers	St Paul
Radiologists	St Michael
Road workers	St John the Baptist
Sailors	St Andrew
	St Brendan
Shepherds	St Bernadette
Shoemakers	St Crispin
	St Crispinian
Social workers	St Louise de Marillac
Soldiers	St George

Students	St Thomas Aquinas
Tailors	St Homobonus
Tax collectors	St Andrew
Teachers	St Gregory the Great
Telecommunications Workers	St Gabriel the Archangel
Tentmakers	St Paul
Tin miners	St Joseph of Arimathea
Weavers	St Barnabas
Winegrowers	St Morand
	St Vincent

The Symbols of the Saints

Blessed Virgin Mary	White lily, rose, pierced heart, crescent moon, twelve stars
St John the Baptist	Lamb, a head on a plate
St Joseph	Depicted with Mary and the infant Christ, lily, tools of a carpenter such as a square
St Mary Magdalene	Alabaster jar of ointment, long hair

The Twelve Apostles

St Andrew	Saltire cross
St Bartholomew (called Nathaniel in the Gospel of St John)	Flaying knives
St James the Greater	Shells, pilgrim's hat and staff
St James the Lesser	Saw
St John	Eagle, chalice with dragon
Judas Iscariot	Pieces of silver and rope
St Jude	Ship, book
St Matthew	Bags of money, spear
St Matthias	Axe
St Peter	Keys
St Philip	Bread, cross
St Simon	Fish, boat, book
St Stephen	Stones
St Thomas	Spear, square

St Acathius	Crown of thorns
St Agatha	Breasts on a plate
St Agnes	Lamb

St Anne (Mother of the Blessed Virgin Mary)	Red robe, doorway
St Anthony the Abbot	Pig, bell
St Anthony of Padua	The infant Christ
St Apollonia	Pincers for pulling teeth
St Augustine of Hippo	Dove
St Bernard of Clairvaux	Bees
St Blaise	Candle, wool comb
St Boniface	Oak
St Bridgit of Sweden	Pilgrims staff and book
St Catherine of Alexandria	Wheel
St Cecilia	Organ
St Christopher	Holding a staff, carrying a child on his shoulders
St Clement	Anchor
St Cosmas & St Damian	Surgical instruments
St Crispin & St Crispinian	Shoes
St Cuthbert	Otters
St David	Harp
St Denis	Carrying his own head
St Dominic	Star, Rosary
St Dorothy	Apples
St Edward the Confessor	Gold ring
St Edmund	Arrow, wolf
St Erasmus	Windlass
St Francis of Assisi	Birds, animals and stigmata
St Francis Xavier	Bell, crucifix
St Gabriel the Archangel	Trumpet

St George	Red cross on shield, Soldier or Knight on horseback Spearing a dragon
St Giles	Deer, Benedictine habit
St Gregory the Great	Crozier, dove
St Helena	Cross
St Hugh of Lincoln	Swan
St Ignatius of Loyola	Cross, book, eucharist
St Isidore	Bees, book and pen
St Jerome	Lion
St Joseph of Arimathea	Silver cruets containing the sweat and blood of Christ
St John the Evangelist	Eagle
St Kentigern	Salmon with ring
St Kevin	Blackbird
St Lawrence	Gridiron
St Lucy	Eyes placed on a dish, lantern
St Luke the Evangelist	Ox, paint brush and palette
St Matthew the Evangelist	Angel
St Margaret	Dragon
St Mark the Evangelist	Winged lion
St Martha	Ladle
St Martin of Tours	A cloak cut in two, geese, globe of fire
St Michael Archangel	Weighing scales, sword, armour, trampling the devil or a dragon underfoot
St Nicholas	Three purses or balls
St Olaf	Crown, dagger
St Oswald	Raven
St Patrick	Serpent, shamrock
St Paul	Sword, book

St Raphael	Fish
St Rock	Dog
St Quentin	Seven-pointed star
St Samson of Dol	Slaying a dragon
St Sebastian	Arrows
St Swithun	Rain
St Teresa of Lisieux	Crucifix entwined with roses
St Thomas Aquinas	Star
St Thomas More	Axe
St Veronica	Veil or handkerchief bearing the image of Christ
St Vincent of Saragossa	Vine
St Vitus	Cross
St Zeno	Crozier, fish
St Zita	Broom

Saints Associated with British Locations

Blessed Virgin Mary	Walsingham, Norfolk
St Aidan	Lindisfarne
St Alban	St Albans, Hertfordshire
St Andrew	St Andrew's, Scotland
St Asaph	St Asaph, Clwyd, Wales
St Austell	St Austell, Cornwall
St Chad	Lichfield, Staffordshire
St Columba	Iona, Argyll, Scotland
St Cuthbert	Durham, County Durham
St David	St David's, Dyfed, Wales
St Eata	Atcham, Shropshire
St Edward the Confessor	Westminster Abbey, London
St Edmund	Bury St Edmund, Suffolk
St Erkenwald	Barking, Essex
St Etheldreda	Ely, Cambridgeshire
St George	Windsor, Berkshire
St Germanus	St Germans, Cornwall
St Giles	Edinburgh, Scotland
St Gwyn	Wrexham, Clwyd, Wales
St Hilda	Whitby, North Yorkshire
St Hugh	Lincoln, Lincolnshire
St Ia	St Ives, Cornwall
St Ives	St Ives, Cambridgeshire
St Joseph of Arimathea	Glastonbury, Somerset
St Melaine	Mullion, Cornwall
St Michael	Skellig Michael, Co Kerry, Ireland
	St Michaels Mount, Cornwall
St Milburga	Wenlock, Shropshire
St Neot	St Neot, Cornwall

St Osmund	Salisbury, Wiltshire
St Osyth	St Osyth, Essex
St Patrick	Armagh, Co Armagh
St Petroc	Padstow, Cornwall
St Richard	Chichester, West Sussex
St Swithun	Winchester, Hampshire
St Thomas Becket	Canterbury, Kent
St Werburga	Chester, Cheshire
St William	York, Yorkshire
St Winifrede	Shrewsbury, Shropshire

Patron Saints of Countries, Regions, Cities and Towns

Albania	Blessed Virgin Mary
Amalfi, Italy	St Andrew
Aragon, Spain	St Braulio
Argentina	Blessed Virgin Mary
Barcelona, Spain	St Eulalia
Bergen, Norway	St Sunniva
Berlin, Germany	St Nicholas
Brazil	St Peter of Alcantara
Brittany, France	St Ivo of Kermartin
Budapest, Hungary	St Stephen of Hungary
Cappadocia, Turkey	St George
Catalonia	St George
Cologne, Germany	St Cunibert
Corfu, Greece	St Spiridon
Cornwall, England	St Petroc
Corsica	St Devota
Crete, Greece	St Titus
Cuba	Blessed Virgin Mary
Denmark	St Anskar
England	St George
Ethiopia	St George, St Frumentius
Egypt	St Mark
Europe	St Benedict, St Cyril, St Methodius
Finland	St Henry of Finland
Florence, Italy	St John the Baptist
France	St Joan of Arc
Germany	St Boniface
Genoa, Italy	St George
Georgia	St George, St Nino
Gibraltar	St Bernard of Clairvaux

Greece	St Paul
Holland	St Willibrord
Hungary	St Stephen of Hungary
Iceland	St Anskar
Ireland	St Patrick
Istanbul, Turkey (Constantinople)	St George, St John Chrysostom, St Roch
Italy	St Francis of Assisi, St Catherine of Siena
Jersey	St Helier
Lithuania	St Hyacinth, St Casimir
Lourdes, France	St Bernadette of Lourdes
Luxembourg	St Willibrord
Macedonia, Greece	St Demetrius
Madagascar	St Vincent de Paul
Majorca, Spain	St Alphonsus Rodriguez
Malta	St Paul
Marseilles, France	St Victor
Menorca, Spain	St Anthony of Egypt
Monaco	St Devota
Moscow, Russia	St George
New Zealand	Blessed Virgin Mary
Norway	St Magnus
Orkney Islands, Scotland	St Magnus
Padua, Italy	St Antony of Padua
Palermo, Sicily	St Benedict the African
Palestine	St George
Pamplona, Spain	St Fermin
Paris, France	St Denis
Patmos, Greece	St John the Evangelist
Peru	St Joseph, St Rose of Lima
Portugal	St Antony of Padua, St George

Ravenna, Italy	St Apollinare
Rome, Italy	St Peter & St Paul
Russia	St Nicholas
Salerno, Italy	St Matthew
Santiago, Spain	St James the Greater
Sardinia	St Maurice
Scotland	St Andrew
Serbia	St Sava, St Demetrius
Spain	St James the Great
Sweden	St Bridget
Switzerland	St Nicholas of Flue
Thessaloniki, Greece	St Demetrius
Turin, Italy	Blessed Virgin Mary
Turkey	St John the Evangelist
USA	Blessed Virgin Mary
Utrecht, Holland	St Willibrord
Venezuela	Blessed Virgin Mary
Venice, Italy	St Mark
Verona, Italy	St Zeno
Vietnam	St Joseph
Wales	St David

Saints and Health Problems

Traditionally saints have been prayed to as intercessors between people and God for many reasons including, importantly, illnesses and health issues. Below is a selection of saints and the maladies and problems they are believed to be especially effective at relieving.

Ague	St Petronilla
Arthritis	St James the Greater
Asthma	St Aldric
Black Death	Fourteen Holy Helpers:
	St Acacius
	St Barbara
	St Blaise
	St Catherine of Alexandria
	St Christopher
	St Cyricus
	St Denys
	St Erasmus
	St Eustace
	St George
	St Giles
	St Margaret of Antioch
	St Pantaleon
	St Vitus
Blindness	St Raphael
Cholera	St Roch
Colic	St Agapitus
Coughing	St Quentin
Cramps	St Maurice
Deafness	St Francis of Sales
Depression	St Columban

Epilepsy	St Vitus
	St Dymphna
Eczema	St Anthony Abbot
Ergotism	St Anthony Abbot
Eye disease	St Lucy
Gallstones	St Florentius
	St Benedict
Gout	St Quirinus
	St Tropez
Headaches	St Acacius
Hernia	St Cathal
Infertility	St Antony of Padua
Leprosy	St Giles
	St George
Lumbago	St Lawrence
Plague	St Gregory the Great
	St Sebastian
Rabies	St Gildas
Rheumatism	St James the Greater
Scrofula	St Marculf
Sore Eyes	St Claire of Assisi
Syphilis	St George
Stomach ache	St Emerentiana
Tuberculosis	St Teresa of Lisieux
Venereal disease	St Fiacre

Web Pages

www.catholic.org/saints
www.catholic-forum.com/saintspatron
www.vatican.va/news_services/liturgy/saints/index_sents_
en.html
www.carr.org/~meripper/saints
www.cin.org/saints.html
www.geocities.com/sufisaints/sufi-mystic.net/text2.htm

Bibliography

The Holy Bible: New Revised Standard Edition, Oxford: Oxford University Press, 1995

Bentley, James, *A Calendar of Saints*, London: Tiger Books, 1997

Burl, Aubrey, *A Guide to the Stone Circles of Britain, Ireland and Brittany*, London: Yale University Press, 1995

Burstein, Dan & De Keijzer, Arne, *Secrets of Mary Magdalene*, London: Weidenfeld & Nicolson, 2006

Cope, Julian, *The Megalithic European*, London: Element Books, 2004

Dowling, Jeremy, *Church Trails in Cornwall: The Liskeard Area*, Truro: North Cornwall Heritage Coast & Countryside Service, 1999

Duffy, Eamon, *The Stripping of the Altars*, New Haven: Yale University, 1992

Farmer, David, *Oxford Dictionary of Saints*, Oxford: Oxford University Press, 2003

Gardner, Laurence, *The Magdalene Legacy*, London: Element Books, 2005

Haskins, Susan, *Mary Magdalen: Myth and Metaphor*, London: HarperCollins, 1993

Hopper, Sarah, *To Be a Pilgrim: The Medieval Pilgrimage Experience*, Stroud: Sutton Publishing, 2002

Jenkins, Simon, *England's Thousand Best Churches*, London: Penguin, 2000

Kanitkar, VP & Cole, W Owen, *Hinduism*, London: Hodder Headline, 2003

Kelly, Sean & Rogers, Rosemary, *Saints Preserve Us!*, London: Robson Books, 1995

Norwich, John Julius, *Byzantium: The Early Centuries*, London: Penguin, 1990

Riches, Samantha, *St George: Hero, Martyr & Myth*, Stroud: Sutton Publishing, 2005

Sanders, EP, *Paul: A Very Short Introduction*, Oxford: Oxford University Press, 2001

Savage, Anne, *The Anglo-Saxon Chronicles*, London: Greenwich Editions, 2002

Taylor, Richard, *How to Read a Church*, London: Rider Publishing, 2004

Voragine, Jacobus de, *The Golden Legend*, London: Penguin, 1998

Walsh, Michael, *Butler's Lives of the Saints*, London: Burns & Oates, 1985

Westwood, Jennifer & Simpson, Jacqueline, *The Lore of the Land*, London: Penguin, 2005

Index

Index

Insulæ